Slow Cookers 2

Published in 2011 by Murdoch Books Pty Limited

Murdoch Books Pty Ltd
Pier 8/9, 23 Hickson Road,
Millers Point NSW 2000
Phone: + 61 (0) 2 8220 2000
Fax: + 61 (0) 2 8220 2558
www.murdochbooks.com.au

Murdoch Books UK Limited
Erico House, 6th Floor
93–99 Upper Richmond Road
Putney, London SW15 2TG
Phone: +44 (0)20 8785 5995
Fax: +44 (0)20 8785 5985
www.murdochbooks.co.uk

Chief Executive: Bruce Hallett
Publishing Director: Chris Rennie

Publisher: Lynn Lewis
Design concept and illustrations: Heather Menzies
Project Manager: Liz Malcolm
Designer: Kyle Mulquin
Production: Renee Melbourne
Recipes developed in the Murdoch Books Test Kitchen

National Library of Australia Cataloguing-in-Publication Data
Slow cookers 2: 100 new recipes, all in one pot.
978-1-74266-383-8 (pbk.)
Includes index. Electric cooking, slow.
641.5884

Printed by Leo Paper Group.
PRINTED IN CHINA

IMPORTANT: Those who might be at risk from the effects of salmonella poisoning (the elderly, pregnant women, young children and
those suffering from immune deficiency diseases) should consult their doctor with any concerns about eating raw eggs.

CONVERSION GUIDE: You may find cooking times vary depending on the oven you are using.
For fan-forced ovens, as a general rule, set the oven temperature to 20°C (35°F) lower than indicated in the recipe.

Slow Cookers 2

100 new recipes, all in one pot

MURDOCH BOOKS

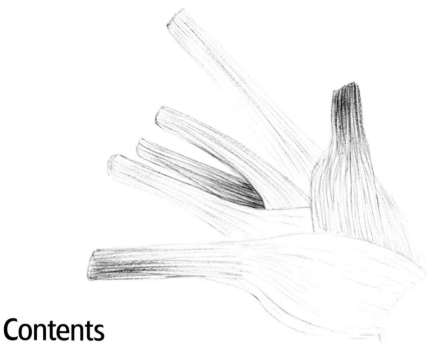

Contents

Hearty family fare

Trends come and go, and when it comes to kitchen gadgetry, we've possibly seen them all. From omelette makers, ice-cream machines and bread makers to plug-in tagines and electric tin openers, it seems there's been an electrical appliance invented for every culinary situation imaginable. Yet how many of us have succumbed to the latest, greatest gizmo, only to discover that it takes up too much space in our cupboards or is annoyingly hard to clean? Having said that, there are some machines and appliances we'd rather not live without. Food processors, blenders and electric beaters have removed a great deal of tedious elbow grease from much of our cooking and we'd be hard pressed to cook successfully without them. Slow cookers are another indispensable kitchen device that no busy household should be without. They've been around since the 1960s and have always had their devotees, but more and more cooks are wising up to the time- and budget-saving capabilities of the slow cooker.

Slow cookers transform many foods (particularly those tougher, tastier cuts of meat) from their raw state to melting tenderness, with not much more exertion than flicking a switch. They can be plugged in anywhere, they use less electricity than your oven, and there is only one bowl to wash up afterwards. You don't need to stir or hover over a meal simmering in a slow cooker and it's almost impossible to burn anything; there's such latitude in cooking times that an hour or two more isn't going to make much difference. In a slow cooker, meals practically cook themselves and they taste incredible — every last drop of the food's natural flavour is captured inside the cooker.

From hearty soups such as curried chicken and peanut to creamy meatballs, catalan beef stew and Thai chilli basil pork ribs, the hardest thing about using your slow cooker will be deciding what to make in it. Slow cookers are also called 'Crock Pots'; Crock Pot is a brand name that was conjured up in America in 1971. Essentially, a slow cooker is an electrical appliance, comprising a round, oval or oblong cooking vessel made of glazed ceramic or porcelain. This is surrounded by a metal housing, which contains a thermostatically controlled element. The lid, which is often transparent, makes it easy to check the progress of what's cooking inside. The recipes in this book were developed using a 4.5 litre (157 fl oz/18 cup) slow cooker but they come in a variety of sizes, with the largest having a capacity of around 7 litres (245 fl oz/28 cups). Note that slow cookers work best when they are at least half, and preferably three-quarters, full (the operating manual that comes with your model will advise you on this).

Most models of slow cookers have a number of temperature settings and typically these are 'low', 'medium' and 'high'. The 'low' setting cooks foods at around 80°C (175°F) while 'high' cooks foods at around 90°C (195°F). 'Medium' is a combination of these two temperatures; when set to medium the slow cooker cooks for around an hour at 'high', then automatically clicks to 'low' and continues cooking at that temperature. As a general rule, cooking on 'low' doubles the cooking time from a 'high' setting and you can tweak the cooking times of recipes to longer or shorter. Recipe cooking times vary from three to 12 hours.

At its simplest, to use your slow cooker all you need to do is prepare and chop your ingredients, add liquid (water, wine or stock) and turn it on, leaving the contents to murmur away until cooked to lush tenderness. Time-strapped cooks can put ingredients in the slow cooker before work and return home at night to a dinner ready-to-go; or, meals can be cooked overnight. The cooking environment in a slow cooker is very moist, making it perfect for tough cuts of meat such as beef blade, lamb or veal shanks, or pork belly. Such cuts contain a great quantity of connective tissues and these can only be broken down with long, slow cooking. When preparing meat, it is important that you trim fatty meat well, as the fat tends to settle on top of the juices.

The slow cooker requires less liquid than normal stovetop or oven cookery, as there is no chance for the liquid to evaporate. In fact, many

Introduction

foods, including some meats, release moisture of their own during cooking (up to one cup per average recipe), so bear this in mind when you think a recipe doesn't have enough liquid in it, or when adapting recipes for the slow cooker (when adapting standard recipes for the slow cooker cut the liquid by 50 per cent). Resist the urge to lift the lid during cooking, particularly at the beginning, as the slow cooker takes a while to heat up, and always cook with the lid on unless the recipe instructs otherwise — perhaps when thickening a sauce. If you need to remove the lid to stir or to check the food is cooked, replace the lid quickly so the slow cooker doesn't lose too much heat.

It is difficult to overcook tougher meats but it is possible (the meat will turn raggedy and fall apart into thin shreds) so you still need to use the suggested cooking times for each recipe. Keep in mind, however, that cooking times may vary, depending on the brand and size of slow cooker you are using. And, because cooking times are fairly approximate, we have rounded our cooking times to the nearest 15 minutes.

While most recipes use the slow cooker as a true one-pot solution, where everything goes in together at the start, other recipes use the cooker as the primary mode of cooking but use other steps along the way. Optionally you can brown meats such as pork, beef or lamb on the stovetop first, before adding them to the cooker. Meat gains extra flavour when browned, as the outside surfaces caramelise over high temperatures (about $100°C/210°F$) and this cannot be achieved in a slow cooker. Recipes in the entertaining chapter of this book include this extra step but for any meat recipe, you can choose to brown first if you like.

Hard vegetables such as root vegetables can take a very long time to cook, so cut them into smallish pieces and push them to the base of the cooker or around the side, where the heat is slightly greater. Green vegetables can lose some nutrients if cooked for prolonged periods, so blanch them first (if required) and add them at the end of cooking to heat through. Seafood and dairy products should also be added to the slow cooker near the end of cooking.

Food safety

In the past there have been concerns about food safety issues with slow cookers, namely whether harmful bacteria that are present in foods, particularly in meats, are killed at such low temperatures. However, bacteria are killed off at around 68°C (155°F), so users of slow cookers need not be concerned about bacteria. One rule here though is to never place meats that are still frozen, or partially frozen, in a slow cooker as this scenario can cause food-poisoning bacteria to flourish; ALWAYS have meats thawed fully before cooking. And never use the ceramic insert after it has been frozen or refrigerated as the sudden change in temperature could cause it to crack.

Another caveat is that you cannot cook dried red kidney beans from their raw state in the slow cooker because the temperature is not high enough to destroy the natural toxins found in these beans. Dried red kidney beans, and other dried beans, need to be boiled for 10 minutes to destroy these toxins. Tinned beans however are safe for immediate use. To prepare dried beans, soak the beans in water for 5 hours or overnight. Discard the water, then rapidly boil the beans in fresh water for 10 minutes to destroy the toxins.

* Make sure you read the manufacturer's instructions for the safe use of your slow cooker.

Soups

Satisfying and sustaining, these meals in a bowl are simplicity itself. Creamy or spicy, thick or thin, there's something for everyone.

CURRIED CAULIFLOWER AND RED LENTIL SOUP

preparation time 15 minutes
cooking time 3 hours
serves 6–8

1 kg (2 lb 4 oz) cauliflower
1 large onion
2 celery stalks
100 g (3½ oz/½ cup) red lentils
1½ tablespoons mild curry paste

400 ml (14 fl oz) tin coconut milk
1 litre (35 fl oz/4 cups) good-quality
  vegetable stock
2 tablespoons finely shredded mint
lime wedges, to serve

● Cut the cauliflower, onion and celery into 2 cm (¾ inch) chunks. Place in a slow cooker with the lentils. In a small bowl, mix the curry paste with the coconut milk until smooth. Pour into the slow cooker, then pour in the stock.

● Cover and cook on high for 3 hours, or until the vegetables are tender.

● Remove and reserve a large ladleful of the cooked cauliflower. In a blender or food processor, blend the remaining soup in several batches until smooth. Season to taste with sea salt and freshly ground black pepper.

● Ladle the soup into serving bowls. Top with the reserved cauliflower florets and the mint and serve with lime wedges.

CREAM OF PARSNIP SOUP

preparation time 20 minutes
cooking time 4 hours 20 minutes
serves 4–6

1 kg (2 lb 4 oz) parsnips, peeled
and chopped
200 g (7 oz) all-purpose potatoes,
such as sebago, peeled and
chopped
1 granny smith apple, peeled, cored
and chopped

1 onion, finely chopped
1 garlic clove, chopped
750 ml (26 fl oz/3 cups) good-quality
chicken stock
a pinch of saffron threads
250 ml (9 fl oz/1 cup) cream
snipped chives, to serve

- Place the parsnip, potato, apple, onion, garlic, stock and saffron threads
in a slow cooker.

- Cover and cook on high for 4 hours.

- Transfer the mixture to a food processor or blender, in batches if necessary.
Purée to a soup consistency, then season to taste with sea salt.

- Return the soup to the slow cooker and stir in the cream. Cover and cook
for a further 20 minutes.

- Ladle the soup into serving bowls. Serve sprinkled with chives and plenty
of freshly ground black pepper.

note *For a vegetarian soup, replace the chicken stock with vegetable stock. For a sensational
dinner party starter, serve this soup topped with pan-fried scallops.*

SPICED CARROT SOUP WITH CORIANDER PESTO

preparation time 20 minutes
cooking time 8 hours 5 minutes
serves 6

2 tablespoons olive oil
1 red onion, diced
1 garlic clove, finely chopped
1 teaspoon cumin seeds
1 teaspoon paprika
1 teaspoon garam masala
3 small red chillies, seeded and
  finely chopped
6 large carrots, peeled and chopped
1 kg (2 lb 4 oz) sweet potatoes,
  peeled and diced
2 large desiree potatoes, peeled
  and diced

1.5 litres (52 fl oz/6 cups)
  good-quality chicken stock
300 ml (10½ fl oz) coconut cream
toasted naan bread, to serve

CORIANDER PESTO

45 g (1½ oz/¼ cup) cashew nuts
1 large handful coriander (cilantro)
  leaves
1 small garlic clove, halved
60 ml (2 fl oz/¼ cup) coconut milk
60 ml (2 fl oz/¼ cup) olive oil

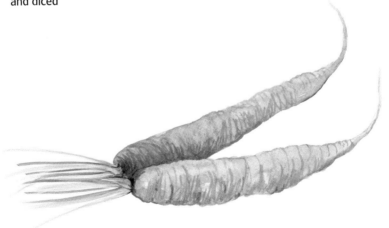

• Heat the olive oil in a frying pan over medium−high heat. Add the onion and garlic and cook, stirring often, for 2−3 minutes, or until the onion has softened. Stir in the spices and chilli and cook for a further 1 minute, or until aromatic.

• Spoon the onion and garlic mixture into a slow cooker and add the chopped vegetables and stock. Mix together well.

• Cover and cook on low for 8 hours.

• Meanwhile, near serving time, make the coriander pesto. Place the cashews, coriander, garlic and coconut milk in a food processor and process until the nuts are finely chopped. With the motor running, gradually add the olive oil in a thin steady stream until well combined.

• Using a stick blender, purée the soup until smooth. Stir the coconut cream through, then season to taste with sea salt and freshly ground black pepper.

• Ladle the soup into serving bowls. Swirl some of the pesto over the top and serve with toasted naan bread.

Note *Garam masala is a blend of ground spices — typically including pepper, mace, cloves, cumin, coriander, cinnamon, cardamom and fennel — that is widely used in Indian cooking to enhance spicy dishes. It is available from supermarkets.*

TUNISIAN CHICKPEA AND SILVERBEET SOUP

preparation time 15 minutes
cooking time 3 hours 40 minutes
serves 4

1 tablespoon olive oil
1 onion, finely sliced
1 teaspoon ground white pepper
1 teaspoon freshly grated nutmeg
½ teaspoon ground cumin
¼ teaspoon ground cloves
¼ teaspoon ground cinnamon
2 x 400 g (14 oz) tins chickpeas,
    rinsed and drained

1 bunch silverbeet (Swiss chard),
    about 900 g (2 lb)
625 ml (21½ fl oz/2½ cups)
    good-quality chicken or
    vegetable stock
Greek yoghurt, to serve
crusty bread, to serve
lemon wedges, to serve

- Heat the olive oil in a frying pan over medium–high heat. Add the onion and cook for 3 minutes, or until it starts to brown, stirring occasionally. Reduce the heat to low and cook for another 5 minutes, or until the onion is soft.

- Add the white pepper, nutmeg, cumin, cloves and cinnamon and continue to cook, stirring, for another 30 seconds. Add the chickpeas and stir until they are well coated in the spiced onion. Transfer the mixture to a slow cooker.

- Wash the silverbeet leaves well and shake dry. Remove the stem below the leaf and discard. Slice across the leaves and stems, cutting the silverbeet into 2 cm (¾ inch) ribbons. Add the silverbeet to the slow cooker and pour in the stock. Gently mix together.

- Cover and cook on low for 2½–3½ hours, or until the silverbeet is just tender.

- Using a stick blender, process the soup in a few short bursts, just to blend a portion of the soup, but not to make it smooth — most of the chickpeas should still be whole. Season to taste with sea salt and freshly ground black pepper.

- Ladle the soup into serving bowls and top with a small dollop of yoghurt. Serve with crusty bread and lemon wedges.

WHITE BEAN AND ROCKET SOUP WITH BASIL PESTO

preparation time 15 minutes
cooking time 8 hours 20 minutes
serves 6

1 large onion, chopped
2 garlic cloves, crushed
2 x 400 g (14 oz) tins cannellini
    beans, rinsed and drained
300 g (10½ oz/2 bunches) rocket
    (arugula), trimmed and chopped
2 litres (70 fl oz/8 cups) good-quality
    chicken stock
125 ml (4 fl oz/½ cup) cream

crusty bread, to serve

BASIL PESTO
2 tablespoons pine nuts, toasted
1 garlic clove, crushed
125 g (4½ oz/1 bunch) basil,
    leaves picked
35 g (1¼ oz/⅓ cup) grated parmesan
60 ml (2 fl oz/¼ cup) olive oil

- Place the onion, garlic, beans, rocket and stock in a slow cooker. Gently mix until well combined. Cover and cook on low for 8 hours.

- Using a stick blender, process the soup until smooth, then stir the cream through. Cover and cook for a further 20 minutes, or until warmed through.

- Meanwhile, make the basil pesto. Place the pine nuts, garlic and basil in a food processor and blend until smooth and combined. Add the parmesan and process for a further 1 minute. With the motor running, add the olive oil in a slow steady stream until the pesto is smooth and of a sauce consistency. Season to taste with sea salt and freshly ground black pepper.

- Ladle the soup into large serving bowls. Sprinkle generously with freshly ground black pepper. Add a generous dollop of the basil pesto and serve with crusty bread.

CAULIFLOWER AND ALMOND SOUP

preparation time 20 minutes
cooking time 3 hours
serves 4

1 large leek, white part only, chopped
2 garlic cloves, crushed
1 kg (2 lb 4 oz) cauliflower, cut into
    small florets
2 all-purpose potatoes, such as
    desiree, (about 370 g/13 oz), diced

1.5 litres (52 fl oz/6 cups) good-
    quality chicken stock
75 g (2½ oz/½ cup) blanched
    almonds, chopped
20 g (¾ oz/⅓ cup) snipped chives
pouring cream, to serve

• Put the leek, garlic, cauliflower, potato and stock in the slow cooker.
Cook on high for 3 hours, or until the potato and cauliflower are tender.

• Using a hand-held stick blender, purée the soup with the almonds.
Alternatively, transfer to a food processor and purée until smooth. Stir through
half the chives and season with salt and freshly ground black pepper. Ladle the
soup into bowls, drizzle with cream and garnish with the remaining chives.

Soups

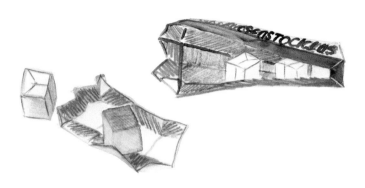

19

RIBOLLITA

preparation time 20 minutes
cooking time 4 hours
serves 6

800 g (1 lb 12 oz) tinned cannellini
   beans, drained and rinsed
400 g (14 oz) tinned chopped
   tomatoes
1 garlic clove, crushed
1 carrot, diced
1 celery stalk, thinly sliced diagonally
¼ cabbage, thinly shredded
300 g (10½ oz) all-purpose potatoes,
   cut into 1 cm (½ inch) dice

2 tablespoons tomato paste
   (concentrated purée)
2 tablespoons extra virgin olive oil
1 litre (35 fl oz/4 cups) good-quality
   chicken stock
200 g (7 oz) 'pane de casa' or crusty
   bread, broken into small chunks
50 g (1¾ oz/½ cup) freshly grated
   parmesan cheese

● Place half the cannellini beans and the tomatoes in the bowl of a food processor. Process until puréed.

● Put the bean and tomato purée in the slow cooker along with the garlic, carrot, celery, cabbage, potato, tomato paste, olive oil and stock. Stir to combine. Cook on high for 4 hours, or until the vegetables are cooked.

● Taste and check for seasoning. Add the remaining cannellini beans, bread chunks and parmesan. Stir and cook for a further 5 minutes, or until the cheese has melted, then serve.

THAI-STYLE PUMPKIN SOUP

preparation time 25 minutes
cooking time 3 hours
serves 4–6

2 butternut pumpkins (squash), about
   3 kg (6 lb 12 oz) in total, peeled,
   seeded and chopped
1 onion, finely chopped
2 kaffir lime leaves, torn
1 lemongrass stem, bruised
1 teaspoon finely grated fresh ginger
1 tablespoon fish sauce
270 ml (9½ fl oz) tin coconut cream

1 tablespoon mild red curry paste
875 ml (30 fl oz/3½ cups)
   good-quality chicken or
   vegetable stock
2 teaspoons lime juice
2 tablespoons Thai sweet chilli sauce
1 small handful coriander (cilantro)
   leaves
1 long red chilli, thinly sliced

● Put the pumpkin and onion in a slow cooker with the lime leaves, lemongrass, ginger and fish sauce. Reserve 2 tablespoons of the coconut cream, then mix the curry paste with the remaining coconut cream until smooth. Pour over the pumpkin mixture, then pour in the stock and gently mix together.

● Cover and cook on high for 3 hours, or until the pumpkin is tender. Set aside to cool slightly. Remove the lime leaves and lemongrass stem.

● Working in batches, transfer the mixture to a food processor and blend until smooth. Stir in the lime juice and sweet chilli sauce and gently reheat, if necessary.

● Ladle the soup into serving bowls and drizzle with the reserved coconut cream. Serve garnished with the coriander and chilli.

HEARTY CHICKEN NOODLE SOUP

preparation time 15 minutes
cooking time 7 hours
serves 4–6

800 g (1 lb 12 oz) chicken breast
  fillets
500 ml (17 fl oz/2 cups) good-quality
  chicken stock
2 celery stalks, diced
1 onion, diced
2 carrots, peeled and diced

1 parsnip, peeled and diced
2 cm (¾ inch) piece of fresh ginger
3 black peppercorns
220 g (7¾ oz) fresh rice noodles
2 zucchini (courgettes), diced
1 handful parsley, finely chopped

• Place the chicken, stock, celery, onion, carrot, parsnip, ginger, peppercorns
and 250 ml (9 fl oz/1 cup) water in a slow cooker. Cover and cook on low for
6 hours.

• Remove the chicken fillets from the slow cooker and allow to cool slightly.
When cool enough to handle, shred the chicken into bite-sized pieces.

• Return the shredded chicken to the slow cooker and stir in the noodles and
zucchini. Turn the slow cooker setting to high and cook for a further 1 hour.

• Discard the ginger and season to taste with sea salt and freshly ground black
pepper. Ladle the soup into deep serving bowls. Sprinkle with the parsley.

CANJA

preparation time 20 minutes
cooking time 3¼ hours
serves 6

3 tomatoes
200 g (7 oz/1 cup) long-grain rice
2.5 litres (87 fl oz/10 cups)
   good-quality chicken stock
1 onion, cut into thin wedges
1 celery stalk, finely chopped

1 teaspoon grated lemon zest
1 mint sprig
2 boneless, skinless chicken breasts
2 tablespoons lemon juice
2 tablespoons shredded mint

• Score a cross in the base of each tomato. Put the tomatoes in a heatproof
bowl and cover with boiling water. Leave for 30 seconds, then transfer to cold
water, drain and peel the skin away from the cross. Cut the tomatoes in half,
scoop out the seeds and chop the flesh.

• Combine the chopped tomatoes, rice, stock, onion, celery, lemon zest and
mint in the slow cooker. Cook on high for 3 hours, or until the rice is tender.

• Prepare the chicken by trimming off any fat, then cutting into thin slices.
Add the chicken to the slow cooker, then add the lemon juice and stir for about
10 minutes, or until the chicken is cooked through. Season to taste with salt
and freshly ground black pepper. Stir in the shredded mint just before serving.

CURRIED CHICKEN AND PEANUT SOUP

preparation time 25 minutes
cooking time 8 hours 20 minutes
serves 4

2 tablespoons fish sauce
2 garlic cloves, crushed
1 tablespoon lime juice
1 tablespoon soft brown sugar
2 small red chillies, seeded if desired,
    finely chopped
1.5 kg (3 lb 5 oz) chicken, rinsed
270 ml (9½ fl oz) tin coconut cream
250 g (9 oz) rice vermicelli noodles
chopped salted peanuts, to garnish
coriander (cilantro) sprigs, to garnish

SPICE PASTE
1 small handful chopped coriander
    (cilantro)
½ small onion, chopped
3 spring onions (scallions), chopped
1 teaspoon grated fresh galangal
1 teaspoon ground turmeric
1 teaspoon ground coriander
2 tablespoons salted peanuts

• Combine the fish sauce, garlic, lime juice, sugar and chilli in a slow cooker. Pour in 750 ml (26 fl oz/3 cups) water and stir until the sugar has dissolved. Add the chicken, placing it breast side down.

• Cover and cook on low for 8 hours.

• Put the spice paste ingredients in a food processor or blender with 2 tablespoons water. Process to a smooth paste.

• Remove the chicken to a plate. Pour the cooking stock from the slow cooker through a sieve into the food processor, then blend with the spice paste until smooth. Return the stock to the slow cooker.

• Discard the skin and bones of the chicken, then shred the meat using your fingers. Stir the shredded chicken through the soup with the coconut cream. Cover and cook for 20 minutes, or until heated through.

• Meanwhile, place the noodles in a large heatproof bowl. Cover with boiling water and leave to soak for 10 minutes, or until softened.

• Drain the noodles and divide among serving bowls. Ladle the soup over the top. Garnish with chopped peanuts and coriander sprigs and serve.

SUKIYAKI SOUP

preparation time 30 minutes
cooking time 2½ hours
serves 4–6

1 teaspoon dashi granules
1 leek, white part only
10 g (¼ oz) dried shiitake mushrooms,
    sliced
1.5 litres (52 fl oz/6 cups)
    good-quality chicken stock
125 ml (4 fl oz/½ cup) soy sauce
2 tablespoons mirin
1½ tablespoons sugar

100 g (3½ oz) Chinese cabbage,
    shredded
300 g (10½ oz) silken firm tofu, cut
    into 2 cm (¾ inch) cubes
400 g (14 oz) rump steak, thinly
    sliced
100 g (3½ oz) dried rice vermicelli
    noodles
4 spring onions (scallions), sliced
    diagonally

• Put the dashi in a heatproof bowl with 500 ml (17 fl oz/2 cups) boiling water
and stir until the granules have dissolved.

• Leave the root attached to the leek and then slice in half lengthways.
Once sliced, wash thoroughly under cold water to remove any grit and then
drain. Thinly slice the leek, discarding the root. Put the dashi, leek, mushrooms,
stock, soy sauce, mirin and sugar in the slow cooker. Cook on low for 2 hours.

• Add the Chinese cabbage and cook for a further 5 minutes, or until wilted.
Stir through the tofu and beef and cook for a further 2 minutes, or until the
beef is cooked through.

• Meanwhile, place the vermicelli in a heatproof bowl, cover with boiling water
and soak for 10 minutes, or until soft, then drain. Divide the noodles among
the serving bowls and ladle on the soup. Serve garnished with the spring onion.

GOULASH SOUP WITH DUMPLINGS

preparation time 30 minutes
cooking time 5¾ hours
serves 6

1 kg (2 lb 4 oz) chuck steak
1 onion, finely chopped
1 garlic clove, crushed
2 tablespoons sweet paprika
pinch cayenne pepper
1 teaspoon caraway seeds
400 g (14 oz) tinned chopped
   tomatoes
750 ml (26 fl oz/3 cups)
   good-quality chicken stock
350 g (12 oz) all-purpose potatoes,

cut into 2 cm (¾ inch) dice
1 green capsicum (pepper), halved,
   seeded and cut into thin strips
2 tablespoons sour cream

DUMPLINGS
80 g (2¾ oz/⅔ cup) self-raising flour
25 g (1 oz/¼ cup) finely grated
   parmesan cheese
2 teaspoons finely chopped thyme
1 egg, lightly beaten

Soups

● Trim the steak of any fat and cut into 1 cm (½ inch) cubes. Put the steak, onion, garlic, paprika, cayenne pepper, caraway seeds, tomatoes, stock and potato in the slow cooker. Cook on low for 4½ hours, or until the beef is tender and the potato is cooked through. Stir in the capsicum, then turn the slow cooker to high and cook for a further 1 hour with the lid off. Season to taste with salt and freshly ground black pepper.

● To make the dumplings, put the flour and parmesan in a bowl. Season with salt and stir in the thyme and egg. Transfer the mixture to a floured surface and lightly knead to a soft dough. Using 1 teaspoon of the mixture at a time, roll it into a ball. Drop the dumplings into the slow cooker. Cover and cook on high for 10–15 minutes, or until the dumplings are cooked through.

● Gently lift the dumplings out of the slow cooker and divide among serving bowls. Stir the sour cream into the soup and ladle the soup over the dumplings.

CALDO VERDE

preparation time 15 minutes
cooking time 4 hours
serves 4

6 all-purpose potatoes, chopped
1 red onion, chopped
2 garlic cloves, crushed
750 ml (26 fl oz/3 cups)
   good-quality vegetable stock

60 ml (2 fl oz/¼ cup) olive oil
1 chorizo sausage (about 180 g/
   6½ oz), diced
500 g (1 lb 2 oz) silverbeet
   (Swiss chard) or kale, thinly sliced

- Put the potato, onion, garlic, stock and olive oil in the slow cooker.

- Cook on high for 3 hours, or until the potato is cooked.

- Using a hand-held stick blender, purée until smooth. Alternatively, transfer to a food processor and blend until smooth. Return to the slow cooker along with the chorizo and silverbeet and cook for a further 1 hour on low. Season to taste with salt and freshly ground black pepper.

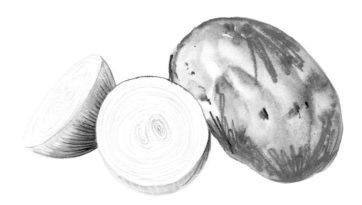

PASTA AND BEAN SOUP

preparation time 30 minutes
cooking time 6½ hours
serves 6

1 onion, finely chopped
1 small celery stalk, finely chopped
1 carrot, finely chopped
1 smoked ham hock, about 500 g
　(1 lb 2 oz), skin scored
400 g (14 oz) tinned chopped
　tomatoes
750 ml (26 fl oz/3 cups) good-quality

　chicken stock
1 bay leaf
1 large rosemary sprig
400 g (14 oz) tinned red kidney
　beans, drained and rinsed
150 g (5½ oz/1 cup) macaroni pasta
2 tablespoons chopped flat-leaf
　(Italian) parsley

• Combine the onion, celery, carrot, ham hock, tomatoes, stock, 1.5 litres
(52 fl oz/6 cups) water, bay leaf and rosemary in the slow cooker.
Cook on low for 6 hours. Remove the ham hock and allow to cool slightly.

• Add the beans and macaroni to the slow cooker. Increase the heat to high
and cook for a further 30 minutes, or until the pasta is al dente.

• When cool enough to handle, remove the meat from the ham hock,
discarding the fat and bone. Cut the meat into small pieces and return to
the slow cooker. Stir through the parsley and season to taste with salt
and freshly ground black pepper. Serve immediately.

Soups

PORK CONGEE

preparation time 15 minutes
cooking time 5 hours
serves 4

300 g (10½ oz/1½ cups) long-grain
   rice, rinsed thoroughly
1 star anise
2 spring onions (scallions), white part
   only, sliced
5 cm (2 inch) piece fresh ginger, thinly
   sliced

2 litres (70 fl oz/8 cups) good-quality
   chicken stock
1 garlic clove, crushed
400 g (14 oz) minced (ground) pork
60 ml (2 fl oz/¼ cup) light soy sauce
white pepper, to season
sesame oil, to serve
fried bread sticks, to serve (optional)

• Put the rinsed rice, star anise, spring onion, ginger slices, stock, 750 ml
(26 fl oz/3 cups) water, garlic and pork in the slow cooker. Cook on low for
5 hours, or until the rice has broken down and is a soupy consistency. Stir
through the soy sauce and season with white pepper.

• Taste and adjust the seasoning with extra white pepper if necessary.
Drizzle with sesame oil and serve with fried bread sticks if desired.

PRAWN GUMBO

preparation time 30 minutes
cooking time 4¼ hours
serves 4–6

1 onion, finely chopped
1 garlic clove, crushed
1 red capsicum (pepper), seeded and
   chopped
4 bacon slices, trimmed of fat, diced
1½ teaspoons dried thyme
2 teaspoons dried oregano
1 teaspoon sweet paprika
¼ teaspoon cayenne pepper
60 ml (2 fl oz/¼ cup) dry sherry

1 litre (35 fl oz/4 cups) good-quality
   fish or light chicken stock
100 g (3½ oz/½ cup) par-cooked
   long-grain rice
2 bay leaves
400 g (14 oz) tinned chopped
   tomatoes
150 g (5½ oz) okra, sliced
1 kg (2 lb 4 oz) raw prawns (shrimp)

Soups

● Put the onion, garlic, capsicum, bacon, thyme, oregano, paprika, cayenne
pepper, sherry, stock, rice, bay leaves, tomatoes and okra in the slow cooker.
Cook on low for 4 hours, or until the rice is cooked and the okra is tender.

● Meanwhile, prepare the prawns. Peel the prawns, leaving the tails intact, then
gently pull out the dark vein from each prawn back, starting at the head end.
Refrigerate until needed.

● Stir in the prawns and cook for a further 15–20 minutes, or until the prawns
are cooked through. Serve immediately.

PRAWN LAKSA LEMAK

preparation time 15 minutes
cooking time 2½ hours
serves 4

4 tablespoons laksa paste
540 ml (19 fl oz) coconut milk
1 tablespoon fish sauce
24 raw king prawns (shrimp), about
    600 g (1 lb 5 oz) in total, peeled
    and deveined, tails left intact
300 g (10½ oz) rice stick noodles

1 cucumber
90 g (3¼ oz/1 cup) bean sprouts, tails
    trimmed
1 large handful coriander (cilantro)
    leaves
1 small handful Thai basil leaves
sambal oelek, to serve

● In a small bowl, mix the laksa paste with the coconut milk. Pour into a slow
cooker, then pour in the fish sauce and 500 ml (17 fl oz/2 cups) water.
Add the prawns and gently mix.

● Cover and cook on low for 2½ hours. Season to taste with sea salt.

● Meanwhile, near serving time, place the noodles in a large heatproof bowl
and cover with boiling water. Leave to soak for 20 minutes, or until softened.

● Meanwhile, cut the cucumber in half lengthways and scrape out the seeds.
Thinly slice the cucumber into matchsticks 5 cm (2 inches) long.

● Drain the noodles and divide among deep serving bowls. Ladle the laksa over
the noodles. Top with the bean sprouts, coriander and basil and serve with the
cucumber and sambal oelek.

*Note Sambal oelek is a spicy condiment made from ground chillies. It is widely used in
Indonesian and Malaysian cooking.*

CORN AND CRAB SOUP

preparation time 10 minutes
cooking time 2 hours
serves 4

420 g (15 oz) tin creamed corn
2 teaspoons grated fresh ginger
2 x 170 g (6 oz) tins crabmeat
6 spring onions (scallions), trimmed
and sliced thinly on the diagonal,
plus extra, to garnish

750 ml (26 fl oz/3 cups) good-quality
chicken stock
1 tablespoon mirin
2 tablespoons soy sauce, plus extra,
to serve
$\frac{1}{4}$ teaspoon ground white pepper
2 egg whites, lightly beaten

- Place the corn, ginger, crabmeat and half the spring onion in a slow cooker.
Pour in the stock, mirin and 500 ml (17 fl oz/2 cups) water.

- Cover and cook on low for 2 hours.

- Stir in the soy sauce and white pepper. Add the egg whites and remaining
spring onion and stir for 1–2 minutes, or until the egg has just cooked through.

- Ladle the soup into serving bowls and sprinkle with extra spring onion.
Serve immediately, with extra soy sauce on the side.

Soups

SALMON TOM KHA

preparation time 30 minutes
cooking time 4 hours 25 minutes
serves 6

1.5 litres (52 fl oz/6 cups) good-
quality chicken stock
4 x 185 g (6½ oz) salmon fillets,
skin and pin bones removed
10 slices fresh galangal
4 large kaffir lime leaves, torn, plus
extra shredded leaves, to garnish
2 x 400 ml (14 fl oz) tins coconut milk
2 tablespoons grated palm sugar
(jaggery)
2 tablespoons fish sauce
175 g (6 oz) oyster mushrooms, sliced
4 small green chillies, split lengthways
80 ml (2½ fl oz/⅓ cup) lime juice
Thai basil leaves, to garnish

**LEMONGRASS AND GALANGAL
PASTE**
2 lemongrass stems, white part only,
finely sliced
5 cm (2 inch) piece of fresh galangal,
peeled and finely chopped
4 coriander (cilantro) roots, washed
well and chopped
5 red Asian shallots, peeled and
chopped
4 garlic cloves, chopped
½ teaspoon white peppercorns
1–2 tablespoons vegetable oil,
if needed

- To make the lemongrass and galangal paste, put the lemongrass and galangal in a small food processor with the coriander root, shallot, garlic and peppercorns. Pulse until broken down and combined, adding the vegetable oil if needed to loosen the mixture.

- Heat a small frying pan over medium heat. Add the lemongrass and galangal paste and cook for 1–2 minutes, or until fragrant. Transfer the paste to a slow cooker.

- Slowly pour in the stock, mixing well. Add the salmon fillets, then scatter the galangal slices and lime leaves over the top.

- Cover and cook on high for 4 hours.

- Remove the salmon fillets and set aside for 10 minutes. When the fish is cool enough to handle, coarsely flake the flesh and set aside.

- Stir the coconut milk, palm sugar and fish sauce into the broth in the slow cooker, mixing well. Return the salmon to the slow cooker and add the mushrooms, chilli and lime juice. Allow to heat through for a further 20 minutes.

- Divide the salmon among deep serving bowls. Ladle the hot broth over the top and garnish with Thai basil and shredded lime leaves.

Home cooking

For family favourites and weekday meals,
the slow cooker helps keep things simple
and easy for the busy cook.

VEGETABLE AND GNOCCHI STEW

preparation time 15 minutes
cooking time 8 hours
serves 4

1 onion, chopped
3 garlic cloves, chopped
2 zucchini (courgettes), cut into 2 cm
   (¾ inch) dice
1 red capsicum (pepper), trimmed,
   seeded and cut into 2 cm (¾ inch)
   dice
100 g (3½ oz) button mushrooms
500 g (1 lb 2 oz) fresh gnocchi

600 ml (21 fl oz) jar tomato passata
   (puréed tomatoes)
500 ml (17 fl oz/2 cups) good-quality
   chicken stock
125 ml (4 fl oz/½ cup) white wine
2 rosemary sprigs
1 small handful chopped basil,
   plus extra sprigs, to garnish
100 g (3½ oz/1 cup) shaved
   parmesan

• Place the onion, garlic, zucchini, capsicum and mushrooms in a slow cooker. Arrange the gnocchi over the top.

• In a bowl, mix together the passata, stock and wine. Pour the mixture into the slow cooker, but do not stir as the gnocchi are quite fragile. Add the rosemary sprigs.

• Cover and cook on low for 8 hours.

• Season to taste with sea salt and freshly ground black pepper and gently stir the basil through. Ladle into serving bowls and scatter the parmesan over the top. Garnish with extra basil sprigs and serve.

CAJUN CHICKEN STEW

preparation time 15 minutes
cooking time 6¼ hours
serves 6

1.5 kg (3 lb 5 oz) chicken thigh fillets,
    trimmed of fat and cut in half
1 tablespoon cajun seasoning
2 tablespoons olive oil
375 ml (13 fl oz/1½ cups)
    good-quality chicken stock
400 g (14 oz) tin chopped tomatoes
1 green capsicum (pepper), seeded
    and cut into 1 cm (½ inch) pieces
2 celery stalks, thinly sliced

1 large onion, diced
60 ml (2 fl oz/¼ cup) worcestershire
    sauce
3 bay leaves
1 teaspoon sugar
1 garlic clove, crushed
1 teaspoon freshly ground black
    pepper
400 g (14 oz/2 cups) basmati rice

● Put the chicken thighs in a large bowl. Sprinkle the cajun seasoning over
them and toss until evenly coated.

● Heat the olive oil in a large frying pan over medium heat. Add the chicken
in batches and fry for 3–4 minutes, or until browned, turning occasionally
and transferring each batch to a slow cooker. Add all the remaining ingredients,
except the rice, to the slow cooker. Mix together well. Cover and cook on low
for 6 hours.

● Meanwhile, near serving time, prepare the rice. Rinse the rice under cold
running water until the water runs clear. Place the rice and 375 ml (13 fl oz/
1½ cups) cold water in a large saucepan, then cover and cook over low heat
for 20–25 minutes, or until the rice is tender.

● Spoon the rice onto serving plates or into wide shallow bowls. Ladle the
chicken mixture over the top and serve.

Home cooking

CHICKEN WITH SATAY SAUCE

preparation time 15 minutes plus overnight marinating
cooking time 6 hours
serves 4

8 chicken thigh fillets, about 1 kg
   (2 lb 4 oz), trimmed of excess fat
290 ml (10 fl oz) tin satay sauce
125 ml (4 fl oz/½ cup) coconut milk
400 g (14 oz/2 cups) jasmine rice
1 tablespoon toasted peanuts,
   chopped
90 g (3½ oz/1 cup) bean sprouts,
   tails trimmed
1 handful coriander (cilantro) sprigs

SOY AND LEMONGRASS MARINADE

2 teaspoons Thai red curry paste
4 garlic cloves, crushed
2 lemongrass stems, white part only,
   chopped
125 ml (4 fl oz/½ cup) soy sauce
1 tablespoon soft brown sugar

● Combine the soy and lemongrass marinade ingredients in a food processor and blend until smooth. Place the chicken thighs in a bowl and pour the marinade over them, tossing to coat. Cover and marinate in the refrigerator overnight.

● Transfer the chicken and the marinade to a slow cooker. Pour the satay sauce and coconut milk over. Cover and cook on low for 6 hours.

● Meanwhile, near serving time, prepare the rice. Rinse the rice under cold running water until the water runs clear. Place the rice in a saucepan with 450 ml (16 fl oz) water. Bring to the boil and boil for 1 minute. Cover tightly, reduce the heat to as low as possible and cook for 10 minutes. Remove from the heat and leave to stand, covered, for 10 minutes.

● When the chicken is done, check the satay sauce for taste and season with sea salt if required. Remove the thighs to a chopping board using tongs or a slotted spoon. Thickly slice each chicken thigh.

● Spoon the rice onto serving plates or into wide shallow bowls, then arrange the chicken over the top. Drizzle the chicken with the satay sauce. Garnish with the peanuts, bean sprouts and coriander and serve.

CHICKEN, PUMPKIN AND HONEY BRAISE

preparation time 20 minutes
cooking time 3 hours
serves 4-6

750 g (1 lb 10 oz) butternut pumpkin
  (squash), peeled, seeded and
  chopped into 2.5 cm (1 inch)
  chunks
1 large onion, chopped
1 kg (2 lb 4 oz) skinless chicken thigh
  fillets

2 tablespoons honey
2 tablespoons honey mustard
250 ml (9 fl oz/1 cup) good-quality
  chicken stock
400 g (14 oz/2 cups) basmati rice
2 tablespoons chopped flat-leaf
  (Italian) parsley

• Place the pumpkin and onion in a slow cooker, then arrange the chicken
on top. In a bowl, mix together the honey, mustard and stock, then pour over
the chicken.

• Cover and cook on high for 3 hours.

• Meanwhile, near serving time, prepare the rice. Rinse the rice under
cold running water until the water runs clear. Place the rice and 375 ml
(13 fl oz/1½ cups) cold water in a large saucepan, then cover and cook
over low heat for 20−25 minutes, or until the rice is tender.

• Just before serving, stir half the parsley through the chicken mixture.

• Spoon the rice onto serving plates or into wide shallow bowls. Ladle the
chicken braise over the top, sprinkle with the remaining parsley and serve.

SPANISH CHICKEN

preparation time 15 minutes
cooking time 3¼ hours
serves 4

6 skinless chicken thigh fillets, about
750 g (1 lb 10 oz) in total
2 chorizo sausages, chopped
1 red onion, chopped
100 g (3½ oz) roasted red capsicum
(pepper) pieces (from a jar), thinly
sliced
4 garlic cloves, finely chopped
1 green chilli, seeded and finely
chopped

2 teaspoons smoked paprika
1 teaspoon dried oregano
400 g (14 oz) tin chopped tomatoes
375 ml (13 fl oz/1½ cups)
good-quality chicken stock
155 g (5½ oz/1 cup) fresh or
frozen peas
crusty bread, to serve

• Trim the chicken thighs of excess fat, then cut into 3 cm (1¼ inch) chunks.

• Place the chicken in a slow cooker with the chorizo, onion, capsicum, garlic, chilli, paprika, oregano, tomatoes and stock. Season with sea salt and freshly ground black pepper and mix together well.

• Cover and cook on high for 3 hours.

• Stir the peas through and cook for a further 15 minutes, or until the peas are warmed through.

• Ladle into serving bowls and serve with crusty bread.

Note *A signature spice in Spanish cuisine, smoked paprika is made from capsicums (peppers) that have been slowly smoked, then ground to a fine powder. It is widely available, but if you don't have any, you can use sweet paprika here.*

Home cooking

CHILLI CHICKEN

preparation time 20 minutes
cooking time 6 hours 20 minutes
serves 4

1 tablespoon chilli flakes
2 teaspoons ground cumin
¼ teaspoon ground cinnamon
60 ml (2 fl oz/¼ cup) olive oil
1.25 kg (2 lb 12 oz) chicken pieces,
    skin on
1 red onion, finely chopped
2 green jalapeño chillies, finely
    chopped
4 garlic cloves, finely chopped
200 ml (7 fl oz) hot taco sauce
125 ml (4 fl oz/½ cup) good-quality
    chicken stock
1 red capsicum (pepper), trimmed,
    seeded and chopped into 2 cm
    (¾ inch) chunks

1 green capsicum (pepper), trimmed,
    seeded and chopped into 2 cm
    (¾ inch) chunks
2 corn cobs, silks and husks removed,
    each cut into thick rounds
400 g (14 oz/2 cups) basmati rice
100 g (3½ oz) whole black olives
1 small handful coriander (cilantro)
    leaves
80 g (2¾ oz/⅓ cup) sour cream
warmed flour tortillas, to serve
    (optional)

- In a small bowl, mix together the chilli flakes, cumin, cinnamon and 2 tablespoons of the olive oil until well combined.

- Place the chicken pieces in a large bowl, add the spice and oil mixture and toss to coat. Rub the spice mixture into the chicken skin with your fingers, making sure the chicken is entirely covered. Season with sea salt.

- Heat the remaining oil in a large frying pan over medium heat. Add the chicken pieces in batches and fry for 10 minutes, turning occasionally, until the skin has browned, transferring each batch to a slow cooker.

- Add the onion, jalapeño chilli, garlic, taco sauce, stock, capsicums and corn to the slow cooker. Mix well to ensure all the ingredients are evenly distributed.

- Cover and cook on low for 6 hours.

- Meanwhile, near serving time, prepare the rice. Rinse the rice under cold running water until the water runs clear. Place the rice and 375 ml (13 fl oz/ 1 ½ cups) cold water in a large saucepan, then cover and cook over low heat for 20–25 minutes, or until the rice is tender.

- Stir the olives through the chicken mixture. Divide among serving plates and sprinkle with the coriander. Serve with the rice and sour cream, and warmed flour tortillas if desired.

Home cooking

CHINESE CHICKEN WITH ALMONDS AND LEMON

preparation time 20 minutes
cooking time 3½ hours
serves 4

2 celery stalks, thickly sliced
2 small carrots, peeled and thickly
    sliced
1 garlic clove, finely chopped
1 cm (½ inch) piece of fresh ginger,
    peeled and sliced into thin strips
375 ml (13 fl oz/1½ cups)
    good-quality chicken stock
1 tablespoon Chinese rice wine
1 teaspoon sesame oil
1 tablespoon cornflour (cornstarch)

2 tablespoons oyster sauce
60 ml (2 fl oz/¼ cup) soy sauce
1 teaspoon caster (superfine) sugar
1 tablespoon lemon juice
600 g (1 lb 5 oz) chicken breast
    fillets, thinly sliced
400 g (14 oz/2 cups) jasmine rice
45 g (1½ oz/½ cup) flaked almonds,
    toasted
thinly sliced spring onions (scallions),
    to garnish

- Place the celery, carrot, garlic, ginger, stock, rice wine and sesame oil in a slow cooker. Cover and cook on high for 3 hours.

- In a large bowl, mix together the cornflour, oyster sauce, soy sauce, sugar and lemon juice until the sugar has dissolved. Add the chicken slices and toss to coat.

- Add the chicken and the sauce mixture to the slow cooker. Cover and cook for a further 30 minutes, or until the chicken is cooked through and the sauce has thickened.

- Meanwhile, near serving time, prepare the rice. Rinse the rice under cold running water until the water runs clear. Place the rice in a saucepan with 450 ml (16 fl oz) water. Bring to the boil and boil for 1 minute. Cover tightly, reduce the heat to as low as possible and cook for 10 minutes. Remove from the heat and leave to stand, covered, for 10 minutes.

- Spoon the rice onto serving plates or into wide shallow bowls, then ladle the chicken mixture over the top. Sprinkle with the almonds and spring onion and serve.

Note *Chinese rice wine is sold in Asian grocery stores and larger supermarkets. If you don't happen to have any, you can always use dry sherry here — but don't be tempted to use a sweet sherry as it will throw the flavours out of balance. To toast flaked almonds, spread them on a baking tray and bake in a preheated 180°C (350°F/Gas 4) oven for 8–10 minutes, or until golden.*

Home cooking

PORCUPINE MEATBALLS

preparation time 10 minutes
cooking time 3 hours.
makes 40 meatballs

500 g (1 lb 2 oz) minced (ground)
   beef
220 g (7¾ oz/1 cup) short-grain rice
1 onion, chopped
1 teaspoon freshly grated nutmeg

2 bay leaves
80 ml (2½ fl oz/⅓ cup)
   worcestershire sauce
420 g (15 oz) tinned tomato soup

● Combine the beef, rice, onion and nutmeg in a bowl and season with salt and freshly ground black pepper. Using about 1½ tablespoons of beef mixture for each, roll the mixture into balls. Cover and chill in the refrigerator overnight.

● Put the meatballs and bay leaves in the slow cooker and cover with the combined worcestershire sauce and tomato soup. Cook on low for 3 hours, or until the meatballs are cooked through.

● Taste the sauce and adjust the seasoning if necessary.
Serve with steamed vegetables.

SAVOURY MINCE

preparation time 10 minutes
cooking time 6¼ hours
serves 6

1 kg (2 lb 4 oz) lean minced
  (ground) beef
2 garlic cloves, crushed
250 g (9 oz/¾ cup) fruit chutney
500 ml (17 fl oz/2 cups) good-quality
  beef stock
3 potatoes, about 800 g (1 lb 12 oz)
  in total, peeled and chopped

2 carrots, peeled and chopped
2 rosemary sprigs
155 g (5½ oz/1 cup) fresh or frozen
  peas
4 tablespoons roughly chopped
  flat-leaf (Italian) parsley
hot buttered toast, to serve

- Place the beef, garlic, chutney, stock, potato, carrot and rosemary
in a slow cooker. Mix together well.

- Cover and cook on low for 6 hours.

- Stir the peas through, then cover and cook for a further 15 minutes,
or until the peas are warmed through.

- Season to taste with sea salt and freshly ground black pepper.
Stir the parsley through and serve with hot buttered toast.

Home cooking

BRAISED TERIYAKI BEEF WITH UDON NOODLES

preparation time 20 minutes

cooking time 8 hours

serves 4

olive oil, for brushing

1 small onion, chopped

375 ml (13 fl oz/1½ cups) teriyaki marinade

125 ml (4 fl oz/½ cup) good-quality beef stock

1 garlic clove, crushed

1.25 kg (2 lb 12 oz) budget rump steaks, cut into 4 cm (1½ inch) chunks

440 g (15½ oz) fresh udon noodles

3 spring onions (scallions), thinly sliced, plus extra, to garnish

ASIAN SALAD

1 small handful coriander (cilantro) leaves

1 red capsicum (pepper), trimmed, seeded and cut into matchsticks

1 large carrot, peeled and cut into matchsticks

1 Lebanese (short) cucumber, seeded and cut into matchsticks

2 tablespoons light soy sauce

1 tablespoon peanut oil

2 tablespoons lime juice

1 teaspoon white sesame seeds

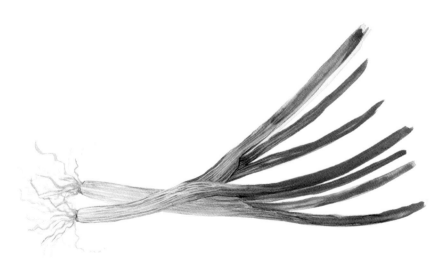

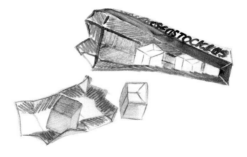

● Lightly brush the bowl of a slow cooker with olive oil. Add the onion to the slow cooker.

● In a large bowl, mix together the teriyaki marinade, stock and garlic. Add the beef to the marinade and toss until well coated. Thread the beef onto 12 small bamboo skewers and place the skewers in the slow cooker.

● Cover and cook on low for 7½ hours, turning the skewers over at least once, if possible.

● Place the noodles in a heatproof bowl and cover with boiling water. Allow to soak for a few minutes, until the noodles have softened.

● Remove the skewers from the slow cooker. Drain the noodles and add to the slow cooker with the spring onion. Stir to coat the noodles with the sauce.

● Place the skewers on top of the noodles, then cover and cook for another 30 minutes, or until the noodles are heated through.

● Meanwhile, near serving time, make the Asian salad. Put the coriander, capsicum, carrot and cucumber in a bowl and toss to combine. Whisk together the soy sauce, peanut oil and lime juice, then pour over the salad. Toss gently and sprinkle with the sesame seeds.

● Serve the skewers on a bed of noodles, sprinkled with extra spring onion. Serve the Asian salad on the side.

STIFATHO

preparation time 20 minutes
cooking time 4¼ hours
serves 4

1 kg (2 lb 4 oz) chuck steak
500 g (1 lb 2 oz) whole baby onions
1 garlic clove, cut in half lengthways
125 ml (4 fl oz/½ cup) red wine
125 ml (4 fl oz/½ cup) beef stock
1 cinnamon stick

4 whole cloves
1 bay leaf
1 tablespoon red wine vinegar
2 tablespoons tomato paste
  (concentrated purée)
2 tablespoons currants

● Trim the beef of excess fat and sinew, then cut into 5 cm (2 inch) cubes. Put beef, onions, garlic, wine, stock, cinnamon stick, cloves, bay leaf, vinegar, tomato paste and some freshly ground black pepper in the slow cooker. Cook on high for 4 hours.

● Stir through the currants and cook for a further 15 minutes. Discard the cinnamon stick and season to taste with salt and extra pepper. Serve with rice, bread or potatoes.

MARMALADE-GLAZED CORNED BEEF

preparation time 15 minutes
cooking time 8 hours
serves 4–6

3 all-purpose potatoes, about 500 g
   (1 lb 2 oz) in total, peeled
80 g (2¾ oz/¼ cup) orange
   marmalade
2 tablespoons dijon mustard
1 tablespoon soft brown sugar

1.5 kg (3 lb 5 oz) corned beef,
   trimmed of excess fat
350 g (12 oz/1 bunch) baby carrots,
   trimmed and peeled
½ small red onion, very thinly sliced
   (optional)
25 g (1 oz/¼ cup) walnut halves
   (optional)

- Cut the potatoes into large chunks and place them in a slow cooker.

- In a small bowl, mix together 2 tablespoons of the marmalade, the mustard
and sugar. Rub the marmalade mixture all over the beef, rubbing it in well. Rest
the corned beef in the slow cooker, on top of the potatoes, and drizzle with any
marmalade mixture remaining in the bowl. Cover and cook for 6 hours on low.

- Add carrots to the slow cooker, then cover and cook for another 2 hours.
Remove the corned beef from the slow cooker and place on a warmed platter.
Cover the meat with foil and set aside to rest in a warm place for 10 minutes
before carving.

- Meanwhile, melt the remaining marmalade. To do this, either warm it in
the microwave in a microwave-safe bowl for about 20 seconds, or place it
in a small saucepan over low heat and cook, stirring, for 1–2 minutes. Brush
the marmalade over the hot beef to glaze it. Carve the beef into thick slices.
Serve with the potatoes and baby carrots, sprinkled with red onion slices and
walnut halves if desired.

Home cooking

BEEF AND VEGETABLE STEW

preparation time 20 minutes
cooking time 4 hours
serves 4

1 onion
1 carrot
1 parsnip
1 swede (rutabaga) or turnip
2 all-purpose potatoes
250 g (9 oz) sweet potato
1 celery stalk
100 g (3½ oz) button mushrooms
2 thick rindless bacon slices, roughly
   chopped

1 kg (2 lb 4 oz) beef blade, skirt steak
   or chuck steak, cut into 4 cm
   (1½ inch) chunks
2 garlic cloves, chopped
1 teaspoon dried oregano
400 ml (14 fl oz) good-quality beef
   or chicken stock
400 g (14 oz) tin chopped tomatoes
2 tablespoons tomato paste
   (concentrated purée)
60 ml (2 fl oz/¼ cup) red wine
1 small handful flat-leaf (Italian)
   parsley, chopped

- Peel the onion, carrot, parsnip, swede, potatoes and sweet potato and cut into 4 cm (1½ inch) chunks. Cut the celery into 4 cm (1½ inch) chunks. Wipe the mushrooms clean and slice in half.

- Put the vegetables in a slow cooker with the bacon and beef. Scatter the garlic and oregano over.

- In a bowl, mix together the stock, tomatoes, tomato paste and wine, then pour over the beef mixture. Season well with sea salt and freshly ground black pepper. Cover and cook on high for 4 hours, or until the meat and vegetables are tender.

- Ladle into serving bowls, sprinkle with the parsley and serve.

VEAL CACCIATORE

preparation time 20 minutes
cooking time 4½ hours
serves 6

1½ tablespoons plain (all-purpose)
    flour
1 kg (2 lb 4 oz) veal osso buco
    (about 6 pieces)
1 onion, chopped
2 garlic cloves, crushed
1 red capsicum (pepper), seeded and
    cut into 2 cm (¾ inch) chunks
1 bay leaf
2 anchovies, chopped
125 ml (4 fl oz/½ cup) good-quality

    chicken stock
400 g (14 oz) tin chopped tomatoes
1 tablespoon tomato paste
    (concentrated purée)
125 ml (4 fl oz/½ cup) white wine
90 g (3¼ oz/½ cup) pitted kalamata
    olives
400 g (14 oz/2 cups) risoni
30 g (1 oz) butter
small handful basil leaves, to serve

● Put the flour in a bowl. Season with sea salt and ground black pepper. Toss the veal lightly in the flour. Place the veal in a slow cooker and sprinkle with any remaining flour. Add the onion, garlic, capsicum and bay leaf.

● In a small bowl, mash the anchovies to a paste using the back of a spoon. Blend with the stock and add to the slow cooker, along with the tomatoes, tomato paste and wine. Cover and cook on high for 4 hours, or until the veal is tender. Remove the lid and cook, uncovered, for a further 30 minutes to thicken the sauce a little. Season the sauce with sea salt and freshly ground black pepper. Stir in the olives.

● Near serving time, add the risoni to a large pot of rapidly boiling salted water and cook according to the packet instructions until al dente. Drain well and stir the butter through. Spoon the risoni into wide shallow serving bowls, then ladle the veal mixture over the top. Sprinkle with the basil and serve.

Home cooking

CREAMY MEATBALLS

preparation time 20 minutes
cooking time 4 hours 20 minutes
serves 4

3 slices (60 g/2¼ oz) day-old crusty
bread, crusts removed
185 ml (6 fl oz/¾ cup) milk
300 g (10½ oz) minced (ground) pork
300 g (10½ oz) minced (ground) beef
60 g (2¼ oz/¼ cup) grated onion
1 teaspoon sea salt flakes
1 teaspoon ground white pepper
1 teaspoon ground coriander seeds
¼ teaspoon ground allspice
2 tablespoons olive oil
125 ml (4 fl oz/½ cup) good-quality
chicken stock
125 ml (4 fl oz/½ cup) cream
1 tablespoon chopped dill, plus extra,
to garnish
finely grated rind of 1 lemon
sliced gherkins (pickles), to serve
(optional)

BEETROOT, ORANGE AND GOAT'S CHEESE SALAD

440 g (15 oz) tin baby beetroot
(beets) in juice, rinsed and drained
1 handful mixed salad leaves
1 blood orange, cut into segments,
peel and all white pith removed
60 ml (2 fl oz/¼ cup) extra virgin olive
oil
1½ tablespoons red wine vinegar
80 g (2¾ oz/⅔ cup) crumbled goat's
cheese

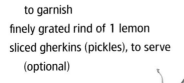

- Roughly chop the bread and place in a bowl. Pour the milk over and set aside to soften for 5 minutes. Squeeze out and discard most of the excess milk.

- In a bowl, combine the bread, pork, beef, onion, sea salt flakes, white pepper, coriander and allspice and mix together well using your hands. Using clean wet hands, form the mixture into 24 meatballs, using about one heaped tablespoon of mixture per ball.

- Heat half the olive oil in a large frying pan over medium–high heat. Add half the meatballs and fry for 3–4 minutes, or until golden all over, turning regularly. Remove to a slow cooker.

- Heat the remaining oil in the pan and brown the remaining meatballs in the same way. Place in the slow cooker. Pour in the stock and cream.

- Cover and cook on low for 3–4 hours, or until the meatballs are cooked through and tender.

- Meanwhile, near serving time, make the beetroot, orange and goat's cheese salad. Wearing gloves, cut the beetroot into quarters and place in a bowl with the salad leaves and orange segments. Whisk together the olive oil and vinegar, season with sea salt and freshly ground black pepper and drizzle over the salad. Gently toss together, then crumble the goat's cheese over the top.

- When the meatballs are cooked, strain the cooking juices into a large frying pan and place over high heat. Cook for 5–10 minutes, stirring regularly, until the liquid has reduced by half and the sauce is very tasty. Stir in the dill.

- Divide meatballs among serving plates or wide shallow bowls, then drizzle the sauce over the top. Sprinkle with the lemon rind and a little extra dill. Serve with the beetroot salad and gherkins, if desired.

Home cooking

GREEK LAMB WITH RISONI AND FETA

preparation time 15 minutes
cooking time 7 hours 40 minutes
serves 4–6

1 kg (2 lb 4 oz) diced lamb
2 small red onions, finely chopped
2 garlic cloves, crushed
2 bay leaves
2 x 400 g (14 oz) tins chopped
  tomatoes
125 ml (4 fl oz/½ cup) good-quality
  chicken stock
125 ml (4 fl oz/½ cup) white wine
220 g (7½ oz/1 cup) risoni
75 g (2½ oz/½ cup) crumbled feta
  cheese
1 tablespoon grated lemon rind
2 tablespoons small oregano leaves
crusty bread, to serve

GREEK SALAD

1 Lebanese (short) cucumber
4 vine-ripened tomatoes, cut into
  wedges
10 kalamata olives
200 g (7 oz/1⅓ cups) crumbled
  Greek feta cheese
60 ml (2 fl oz/¼ cup) extra virgin olive
  oil
1 tablespoon lemon juice

- Put the lamb, onion, garlic, bay leaves and tomatoes in a slow cooker. Pour in the stock and wine and mix together.

- Cover and cook on low for 7 hours, or until the lamb is very tender.

- Sprinkle the risoni over the lamb and mix it in well. Cover and cook for a further 40 minutes, or until the risoni is tender.

- Meanwhile, near serving time, make the Greek salad. Cut the cucumber in half lengthways, discard the seeds, then cut into bite-sized pieces. Place in a serving bowl with the tomato, olives and feta. Whisk together the olive oil and lemon juice, pour over the salad and gently toss together.

- Season the lamb mixture generously with freshly ground black pepper.

- Divide the lamb mixture among wide shallow serving bowls, sprinkle with feta, lemon rind and oregano and serve with the Greek salad and crusty bread.

CHINESE BRAISED LAMB

preparation time 15 minutes plus overnight marinating
cooking time 8 hours
serves 4

60 ml (2 fl oz/¼ cup) hoisin sauce
2 teaspoons finely grated fresh ginger
2 garlic cloves, thinly sliced
2 star anise
1 tablespoon dark soy sauce
1 tablespoon dry sherry
1 tablespoon tomato sauce (ketchup)
1 teaspoon sesame oil

1 kg (2 lb 4 oz) lamb shoulder, boned
   and diced into 4 cm (1½ inch)
   pieces (ask your butcher to do this)
400 g (14 oz/2 cups) jasmine rice
6 spring onions (scallions), thinly
   sliced on the diagonal
steamed Asian greens, to serve

● In a large bowl, mix together the hoisin sauce, ginger, garlic, star anise, soy sauce, sherry, tomato sauce and sesame oil. Add the lamb and toss until well coated. Cover and marinate in the refrigerator overnight if desired.

● Transfer the lamb mixture to a slow cooker, adding all the marinade from the bowl. Cover and cook on low for 8 hours, stirring occasionally.

● Meanwhile, near serving time, prepare the rice. Rinse the rice under cold running water until the water runs clear. Place the rice in a saucepan with 450 ml (16 fl oz) water. Bring to the boil and boil for 1 minute. Cover tightly, reduce the heat to as low as possible and cook for 10 minutes. Remove from the heat and leave to stand, covered, for 10 minutes.

● Spoon the rice onto serving plates or into wide shallow bowls, then ladle the lamb mixture over the top. Drizzle with the cooking juices, sprinkle with the spring onion and serve with steamed Asian greens.

LAMB RAGÙ

preparation time 15 minutes
cooking time 5½ hours
serves 4–6

1 kg (2 lb 4 oz) minced (ground) lamb
400 g (14 oz) tin chopped tomatoes
250 ml (9 fl oz/1 cup) tomato passata
   (puréed tomatoes) or pasta sauce
125 ml (4 fl oz/½ cup) red wine
2 carrots, peeled and diced
2 onions, diced
2 celery stalks, diced
2 tablespoons pesto
2 tablespoons tomato paste
   (concentrated purée)

4 garlic cloves, crushed
1 teaspoon chilli flakes
½ teaspoon dried oregano
1 rosemary sprig
1 thyme sprig
400 g (14 oz) pasta tubes, such as
   penne or rigatoni
1 small handful finely chopped
   flat-leaf (Italian) parsley
50 g (1¾ oz/½ cup) finely grated
   parmesan

• Put the lamb, tomatoes and passata in a slow cooker. Pour in the wine, then add the carrot, onion, celery, pesto, tomato paste and garlic. Sprinkle with the chilli flakes and oregano and add the rosemary and thyme sprigs.

• Cover and cook on low for 5½ hours.

• Meanwhile, near serving time, add the pasta to a large pot of rapidly boiling salted water and cook according to the packet instructions until al dente, about 10 minutes. Drain well.

• Divide the pasta among serving bowls, then spoon the lamb ragù over the top. Sprinkle with the parsley and parmesan and serve.

Home cooking

LAMB MEATBALLS WITH SPICY SAFFRON SAUCE

preparation time 30 minutes plus 30 minutes chilling
cooking time 8¼ hours
serves 4

2 tablespoons olive oil
400 g (14 oz) fresh pappardelle
grated parmesan, to serve
basil leaves, to garnish

MEATBALLS

650 g (1 lb 7 oz) minced (ground)
    lamb
100 g (3½ oz/1 cup) dry breadcrumbs
1 egg, lightly beaten
1 garlic clove, crushed
2 teaspoons dried oregano
½ teaspoon sea salt
½ teaspoon freshly ground black
    pepper
2 tablespoons olive oil

SPICY SAFFRON SAUCE

1 teaspoon saffron threads
115 g (4 oz/¾ cup) blanched
    almonds, toasted
1 garlic clove, crushed
55 g (2 oz/½ cup) ground hazelnuts
2 tablespoons tomato passata
    (puréed tomatoes)
2 tablespoons red wine vinegar
340 g (12 oz) jar roasted red
    capsicum (pepper) strips, drained
2 x 400 g (14 oz) tins chopped
    tomatoes
2 teaspoons paprika
1 teaspoon cayenne pepper
1 teaspoon chilli flakes
2 teaspoons soft brown sugar

• To make the meatballs, combine the meatball ingredients in a large bowl and mix together well using your hands.

• Using clean wet hands, form the mixture into 24 meatballs, using about one heaped tablespoon of mixture per ball. Place the meatballs on a plate, then cover and refrigerate for 30 minutes.

• Meanwhile, make the spicy saffron sauce. In a small bowl, soak the saffron in 2 tablespoons hot water for 5 minutes to infuse.

• Place the almonds and garlic in a food processor and pulse until a smooth paste forms. Add the ground hazelnuts, passata, vinegar, capsicum and one tin of chopped tomatoes and process to a smooth consistency. Add the saffron water, paprika, cayenne pepper, chilli flakes and sugar and pulse until thoroughly mixed. Pour the mixture into a slow cooker.

• Heat the olive oil in a frying pan over medium heat. Add the meatballs in batches and fry for 3–4 minutes each time, or until evenly browned, turning often and transferring each batch to the slow cooker.

• Cover and cook on low for 8 hours.

• Meanwhile, near serving time, add the pasta to a large pot of rapidly boiling salted water and cook according to the packet instructions until al dente. Drain well.

• Divide the pasta among serving bowls. Season the meatball mixture to taste with sea salt and freshly ground black pepper, then spoon the meatballs and sauce over the top. Sprinkle with parmesan and basil leaves and serve.

Home cooking

ROSEMARY AND REDCURRANT LAMB ROAST

preparation time 20 minutes
cooking time 8 hours
serves 6

2.25 kg (5 lb) leg of lamb, trimmed
  of excess fat
1 garlic clove, halved
3 rosemary sprigs, cut in half
160 g (5¾ oz/½ cup) redcurrant jelly,
  melted
½ small pumpkin (winter squash),
  about 650 g (1 lb 7 oz) in total
1 onion

12 new potatoes, about
  900 g (2 lb) in total
1 bay leaf
1 tablespoon olive oil
steamed peas, to serve

- Make six large incisions in the lamb, then rub the lamb all over with the cut garlic. Insert the rosemary sprigs in the incisions. Brush the lamb well with half the redcurrant jelly and season generously with sea salt and freshly ground black pepper.

- Leaving the skin on, remove the seeds from the pumpkin and cut the flesh into 5 cm (2 inch) wedges. Peel the onion and cut into rounds, but do not separate the rings. Scrub the potatoes but leave the skins on. Cut any larger ones in half. Place the potatoes, pumpkin, onion and bay leaf in the slow cooker, then rest the lamb on top. Cover and cook on low for 8 hours.

- Remove the lamb from the slow cooker and place on a warmed platter. Cover with foil and leave to rest in a warm place for 10 minutes before carving.

- Drizzle the vegetables in the slow cooker with the olive oil and season to taste with sea salt and freshly ground black pepper.

- Carve the lamb and divide among serving plates. Serve with the remaining redcurrant jelly, the braised vegetables and peas.

LAMB CHOPS IN RATATOUILLE

preparation time 30 minutes
cooking time 7–7½ hours
serves 4–6

1 kg (2 lb 4 oz) lamb forequarter
  chops
1 eggplant (aubergine), cut into
  2 cm (¾ inch) cubes
1 red capsicum (pepper), cut into
  2 cm (¾ inch) cubes
1 green capsicum (pepper), cut into
  2 cm (¾ inch) cubes
1 red onion, cut into 1 cm (½ inch)
  cubes
2 tablespoons capers
4 anchovies, chopped

80 g (2¾ oz/½ cup) pitted kalamata
  olives, chopped
60 g (2¼ oz/¼ cup) tomato paste
  (concentrated purée)
2 garlic cloves, chopped
400 g (14 oz) tinned chopped
  tomatoes
150 g (5½ oz/¾ cup) Israeli couscous
  (see Note)
1 small handful flat-leaf (Italian)
  parsley, chopped

● Trim the lamb chops of excess fat and cut into pieces. Put the eggplant,
red and green capsicum, onion, capers, anchovies, olives, tomato paste, garlic
and tomatoes in the slow cooker. Put the lamb chops on top. Cook on low for
6–6½ hours, or until the lamb is tender, stirring occasionally.

● Stir in the couscous and continue to cook for another 1 hour, or until the
couscous is tender and cooked through.

● Season with salt and freshly ground black pepper, and sprinkle with parsley
before serving.

Note *Israeli couscous is larger in size than the more familiar Moroccan couscous, and has a
chewier texture. It is sold in most gourmet food stores and health food stores.*

CRYING LEG OF LAMB

preparation time 30 minutes
cooking time 5–6 hours
serves 4

GARLIC RUB
2–3 garlic cloves, crushed
1 tablespoon olive oil
1 teaspoon dried oregano

4 all-purpose potatoes, halved
250 g (9 oz) orange sweet potato,
  cut into 5 cm (2 inch) chunks

150 g (5½ oz) long, thin eggplants
  (aubergines), cut into
  5 cm (2 inch) chunks
2 tomatoes, quartered
1.5 kg (3 lb 5 oz) easy-carve lamb leg
1 tablespoon cornflour (cornstarch)

• To make the garlic rub, mash together the garlic and 1 teaspoon salt in
a small bowl to make a paste. Stir in the olive oil and oregano and season
with plenty of freshly ground black pepper.

• Scatter the potato, sweet potato, eggplant and tomatoes over the base of
the slow cooker. Wash and pat dry the lamb with paper towel, and remove any
excess fat. Rub the garlic paste all over the lamb. Place the lamb in the slow
cooker on top of the vegetables. Cover and cook on low for 5–6 hours,
or until the lamb is cooked to your liking.

• Transfer the lamb to a large plate, cover with foil and leave to rest for
10 minutes. Use a slotted spoon to lift the vegetables from the juice to a
serving plate. Discard the fat from the surface of the juice left in the slow
cooker. Increase the heat to high. Combine the cornflour with 1 tablespoon
water and stir it into the juices. Stir over high heat for 10–15 minutes, or until
thickened, then strain into a jug. Carve the lamb into thick chunks and serve
with the vegetables and thickened juices.

LASAGNE WITH HAM, LEMON AND BASIL

preparation time 25 minutes
cooking time 3 hours
serves 4–6

olive oil, for brushing
690 ml (24 fl oz) jar tomato passata (puréed tomatoes)
2 garlic cloves, crushed
150 g (5½ oz/1¼ cups) grated cheddar cheese
50 g (13/4 oz/½ cup) grated parmesan
1 egg

300 ml (10½ fl oz) thick (double/heavy) cream
1 handful basil, chopped
1 teaspoon grated lemon rind
150 g (5½ oz) shaved ham, shredded
250 g (9 oz) packet instant lasagne sheets
mixed salad leaves, to serve

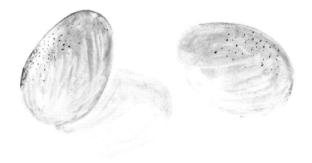

- Lightly brush the bowl of a slow cooker with olive oil.

- In a bowl, mix together the passata and garlic.

- In a separate bowl, mix together 125 g (4½ oz/1 cup) of the cheddar, the parmesan, egg, cream, basil and lemon rind. Season to taste with sea salt and freshly ground black pepper.

- Spoon one-third of the passata mixture into the slow cooker. Top with one-third of the ham and one-quarter of the cheese mixture. Arrange one-third of the lasagne sheets over the top in a single layer.

- Spoon another one-third of the passata mixture over the lasagne sheets, then top with another one-third of the ham and one-quarter of the cheese mixture. Layer another one-third of the lasagne sheets over the top.

- Repeat with the remaining passata, ham, another one-quarter of the cheese mixture and the remaining lasagne sheets to make a third layer. Spread the remaining cheese mixture over the top of the lasagne, ensuring that all the pasta is covered, otherwise it will not cook through properly. Sprinkle with the remaining cheddar.

- Cover and cook on low for 3 hours, or until the pasta is tender. Allow the lasagne to sit for 10 minutes before serving with mixed salad leaves.

CABBAGE ROLLS

preparation time 30 minutes
cooking time 2½ hours
serves 4

½ large cabbage
400 g (14 oz) minced (ground) pork
220 g (7¾ oz/1 cup) par-cooked
    short-grain rice
50 g (1¾ oz/½ cup) seasoned stuffing
    mix or dry breadcrumbs
2 garlic cloves, crushed
1 egg, lightly beaten

1 onion, finely diced
1 tablespoon dijon mustard
1 tablespoon worcestershire sauce
¼ teaspoon white pepper
60 ml (2 fl oz/¼ cup) red wine vinegar
2 bacon slices, thinly sliced
500 g (1 lb 2 oz/2 cups) tomato
    passata (puréed tomatoes)

• Place the cabbage in a large heatproof bowl. Pour over boiling water to cover. Set aside for 5–10 minutes, or until you can separate the cabbage leaves with kitchen tongs. Refresh the leaves in cold water and drain.

• Combine pork, rice, stuffing mix, garlic, egg, onion, mustard, worcestershire sauce, white pepper and 1½ teaspoons salt in a bowl. Add 1 tablespoon of the vinegar.

• Use the larger cabbage leaves to roll the parcels, and set the smaller leaves aside for later use. Cut a 'V' shape to remove the large connecting vein in each cabbage leaf. Form some of the pork stuffing mixture into a sausage shape about 2 cm (¾ inch) thick and 4 cm (1½ inches) long and place it in the middle of the cabbage leaf. Roll the cabbage up around the pork, making sure the filling is completely covered. Continue until all the large leaves are used.

• Thinly shred the small cabbage leaves and place in the slow cooker. Put bacon on top, then the cabbage rolls. Top with tomato passata and remaining vinegar. Cook on high for 2½ hours, or until the pork filling is cooked through.

LION'S HEAD MEATBALLS

preparation time 30 minutes
cooking time 2¼ hours
serves 4

450 g (1 lb) minced (ground) pork
1 egg white
4 spring onions (scallions), finely
   chopped
1 tablespoon Chinese rice wine
1 teaspoon grated fresh ginger
1 tablespoon light soy sauce

2 teaspoons sugar
1 teaspoon sesame oil
white pepper
750 ml (26 fl oz/3 cups) chicken stock
300 g (10½ oz) bok choy (pak choy),
   sliced
100 g (3½ oz) dried rice vermicelli
   noodles

● Put the pork and egg white in a food processor and process briefly until
you have a fluffy mixture. Alternatively mash the pork in a large bowl and
gradually stir in the egg white, beating the mixture well until it is fluffy.

● Add the spring onion, rice wine, ginger, soy sauce, sugar and sesame oil,
season with salt and white pepper, and process or beat again briefly.
Divide the mixture into walnut-sized balls.

● Place the meatballs in the slow cooker, then pour in the stock. Cook on low
for 2 hours. Add the bok choy and cook for a further 10 minutes, or until the
bok choy is wilted.

● Meanwhile, place the vermicelli noodles in a heatproof bowl, cover with
boiling water and soak for 10 minutes, or until soft. Drain the vermicelli and
add them to the slow cooker. Stir to combine. To serve, ladle the vermicelli,
meatballs and some broth into deep bowls.

Home cooking

STICKY PORK RIBS

preparation time 20 minutes
cooking time 4 hours
serves 4–6

olive oil, for brushing
1.25 kg (2 lb 12 oz) pork barbecue
   ribs (not spare ribs)
1 red onion, finely chopped
1 green capsicum (pepper), trimmed,
   seeded and finely chopped
1 green chilli, seeded and finely
   chopped
2 garlic cloves, finely chopped
185 ml (6 fl oz/¾ cup) barbecue
   sauce
2 tablespoons white wine vinegar
2 tablespoons soft brown sugar
1 tablespoon sweet chilli sauce
2 teaspoons worcestershire sauce
a dash of Tabasco sauce
coriander (cilantro) leaves, to garnish
   (optional)
trussed cherry tomatoes, to serve

CORN SALSA
350 g (12 oz/2⅓ cups) frozen corn
   kernels
2 spring onions (scallions), finely
   chopped
1 tablespoon finely chopped
   coriander (cilantro) leaves
1 tablespoon extra virgin olive oil
2 tablespoons lime juice

- Lightly brush the bowl of a slow cooker with olive oil. Cut the ribs into sets of two or three; trim off any excess fat.

- Put the ribs in the slow cooker. Scatter onion, capsicum, chilli and garlic over the ribs. Season well with sea salt and freshly ground black pepper.

- In a small bowl, combine the barbecue sauce, vinegar, sugar, chilli sauce, worcestershire sauce, Tabasco and 60 ml (2 fl oz/¼ cup) water. Mix well to dissolve the sugar, then pour over the ribs.

- Cover and cook on high for 3½ hours, or until the ribs are tender. During cooking, stir the mixture once or twice to keep the ribs covered with the sauce.

- After 3½ hours, check the ribs — the meat should be tender, but not falling off the bone. If the meat isn't yet tender, put the lid back on and continue to cook for another 30 minutes.

- Meanwhile, near serving time, prepare the corn salsa. Bring a saucepan of water to the boil over high heat. Add the corn and cook for 2–3 minutes, or until just tender. Drain well, then place in a bowl. Add the spring onion, coriander, olive oil and lime juice and gently toss to combine.

- Using tongs, remove the ribs to a large serving plate. Skim off any surface fat from the sauce, then spoon some sauce over the ribs. Garnish with coriander if desired. Serve with the corn salsa and cherry tomatoes.

PORK WITH APPLE SAUCE

preparation time 25 minutes
cooking time 5¼ hours
serves 4

1 kg (2 lb 4 oz) boneless pork leg
    roast, trimmed and cut into 4 cm
    (1½ inch) chunks
1 tablespoon rosemary
1 leek, white part only, rinsed well,
    trimmed and chopped
500 g (1 lb 2 oz) sweet potatoes,
    peeled and cut into 3 cm (1¼ inch)
    chunks
1 small fennel bulb, trimmed and
    thickly sliced

100 g (3½/2 oz) button mushrooms,
    halved
1 apple, peeled, cored and chopped
2 garlic cloves, chopped
375 ml (13 fl oz/1½ cups) sparkling
    apple cider
1 tablespoon cornflour (cornstarch)
2 tablespoons chopped flat-leaf
    (Italian) parsley
steamed English spinach, to serve

● Place the pork in a slow cooker. Sprinkle with the rosemary, season well with
sea salt and freshly ground black pepper and gently toss to coat.

● Add the leek, sweet potato, fennel, mushrooms, apple and garlic to the slow
cooker and gently mix together. Pour in the cider. Cover and cook on high for
5 hours, or until the pork is tender.

● Remove the lid. Blend the cornflour with 1 tablespoon water until smooth,
then stir through the pork mixture.

● Cook, uncovered, for a further 15 minutes, or until the sauce has thickened
slightly. Sprinkle with the parsley and serve with steamed spinach.

PORK WITH SUCCOTASH

preparation time 25 minutes
cooking time 4¼ hours
serves 4

1.3 kg (3 lb) pork loin rack,
    with 4 chops
75 g (2½ oz) piece of pancetta,
    about 1 cm (½ inch) thick, chopped
1 red onion, thinly sliced
1 green capsicum (pepper), trimmed,
    seeded and thinly sliced
1 green apple, peeled, cored and
    thinly sliced
2 garlic cloves, finely chopped
4 small rosemary sprigs, plus extra
    leaves, for sprinkling

250 ml (9 fl oz/1 cup) good-quality
    chicken stock
1 tablespoon cornflour (cornstarch)
125 ml (4 fl oz/½ cup) cream
400 g (14 oz) tin butter beans
    (lima beans), rinsed and drained
400 g (14 oz) tin corn kernels,
    drained
2 tablespoons finely chopped flat-leaf
    (Italian) parsley

Home cooking

• Trim the pork rack of skin and excess fat. Season generously with sea salt
and freshly ground black pepper. Place the pork rack in a slow cooker. Scatter
the pancetta, onion, capsicum, apple, garlic and rosemary sprigs over, then pour
in the stock. Cover and cook on high for 4 hours, or until the pork and
vegetables are tender. Using tongs, remove the pork rack to a warmed plate.
Cover with foil and leave to rest in a warm place while finishing the sauce.

• Blend the cornflour with 1 tablespoon water until smooth. Stir the mixture
into the sauce in the slow cooker, together with the cream. Cover and cook for
10 minutes to thicken the sauce a little. Stir in the butter beans, corn kernels
and half the parsley, then cook for a further 5 minutes to warm the beans and
corn. To serve, carve the loin into 4 cutlets and divide among serving plates.
Spoon the vegetables and sauce over. Sprinkle with the remaining parsley and
extra rosemary and serve.

BACON-WRAPPED PORK COOKED WITH MAPLE SYRUP

preparation time 25 minutes
cooking time 8 hours 40 minutes
serves 6

1.25 kg (2 lb 12 oz) piece of pork
   neck, trimmed of any visible fat
6 rindless bacon slices, about
   400 g (14 oz) in total
olive oil, for brushing
2 rosemary sprigs
125 ml (4 fl oz/½ cup) maple syrup
1 tablespoon cornflour (cornstarch)
steamed asparagus, to serve

CREAMY CELERIAC AND POTATO MASH

1 celeriac
1 large roasting potato, such as russet
   or king idaho, peeled and cut into
   2.5 cm (1 inch) chunks
250 ml (9 fl oz/1 cup) milk
20 g (¾ oz) unsalted butter, softened

- Season the pork with sea salt and freshly ground black pepper.

- Cut six lengths of kitchen string, each about 80 cm (32 inches) long. Lay them on a clean work surface, evenly spaced to the width of the pork. Lay the bacon slices so they just overlap on top of the string, and run the same way as the string. Place the pork in the centre of the bacon. Roll up firmly and tie the strings to secure the pork into a roll — the bacon should cover the top of the pork.

- Heat a large non-stick frying pan over high heat. Add the pork and brown for 10 minutes, turning regularly.

- Lightly brush the bowl of a slow cooker with olive oil. Place the rosemary sprigs in the slow cooker and rest the pork on top. Season again with freshly ground black pepper, then pour the maple syrup over.

- Cover and cook on low heat for 8 hours, or until the pork is very tender. Transfer the pork to a warm platter and cover with foil. Leave to rest in a warm place while finishing the sauce.

- Turn the slow cooker setting to high. Blend the cornflour with 1 tablespoon water until smooth, then stir into the sauce. Cover and cook for a further 30 minutes, or until the sauce is slightly thickened.

- Meanwhile, make the celeriac and potato mash. Trim and peel the celeriac, then chop into 2.5 cm (1 inch) chunks. Place in a saucepan with the potato and milk and bring to the boil over high heat. Cover and cook for 15 minutes, or until tender. Mash well and season to taste with sea salt and freshly ground black pepper. Stir in the butter and keep warm.

- Carve the pork into thick slices and drizzle with the sauce from the slow cooker. Serve with the celeriac and potato mash and steamed asparagus.

Entertaining

Cooking something special is a breeze
with no-fuss recipes that ensure the cook
doesn't spend hours in the kitchen.

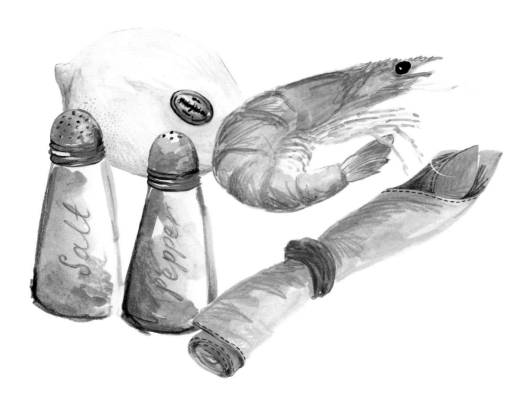

CHICKEN WITH CAPONATA AND BALSAMIC VINEGAR

preparation time 30 minutes
cooking time 6 hours 25 minutes
serves 6

2 tablespoons olive oil

3 anchovy fillets

2 red onions, thinly sliced

2 garlic cloves, crushed

1 red capsicum (pepper), trimmed, seeded and chopped into 1 cm (½ inch) pieces

1 yellow capsicum (pepper), trimmed, seeded and chopped into 1 cm (½ inch) pieces

2 eggplants (aubergines), cut into 1 cm (½ inch) dice

100 g (3½ oz) pancetta, finely chopped

2 vine-ripened tomatoes, chopped

1 tablespoon baby capers, rinsed and drained

1 tablespoon balsamic vinegar

2 teaspoons sugar

1.5 kg (3 lb 5 oz) chicken thighs on the bone, skin removed and trimmed of any fat

1 small handful flat-leaf (Italian) parsley, chopped

steamed green beans, to serve

● Heat half the olive oil in a large heavy-based saucepan over medium heat. Add the anchovies and onion and cook, stirring, for 3 minutes. Remove the onion mixture to a slow cooker.

● Heat the remaining oil in the pan. Add the garlic, capsicum, eggplant and pancetta and sauté for 10–15 minutes, or until the vegetables are tender. Stir in the tomato, capers, vinegar and sugar and simmer for 3–5 minutes.

● Transfer the caponata mixture to the slow cooker. Add the chicken and gently toss to coat well in the caponata. Clean the sides of the cooker with a damp cloth if necessary.

● Cover and cook on low for 5–6 hours, or until the chicken is very tender. Season to taste with sea salt and freshly ground black pepper. Transfer the mixture to serving plates and sprinkle with the parsley. Serve with steamed green beans.

CHICKEN LEG QUARTERS WITH LEMON AND GREEN OLIVES

preparation time 25 minutes

cooking time 7¼ hours

serves 4

2 desiree potatoes, about 500 g
(1 lb 2 oz) in total, peeled and cut
into 2 cm (¾ inch) wedges
8 pickling onions or French shallots,
peeled
8 chicken leg quarters
1 tablespoon olive oil
125 ml (4 fl oz/½ cup) white wine
2 tablespoons lemon juice
200 g (7 oz) green beans, trimmed
90 g (3¼ oz/½ cup) green olives,
pitted
1 large handful flat-leaf (Italian)
parsley, plus extra, to garnish
lemon wedges, to serve

HERB BUTTER
60 g (2¼ oz) butter, softened
3 garlic cloves, crushed
1 tablespoon chopped lemon thyme
1 teaspoon chopped tarragon
60 ml (2 fl oz/¼ cup) lemon juice

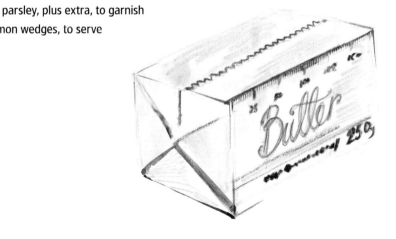

- Place the potato and onions in a slow cooker.

- In a small bowl, mix together the herb butter ingredients until well combined. Use your fingers to gently loosen the skin away from the flesh of each chicken leg quarter, working as far down into the drumstick as you can. Ease the herb butter under the skin. Season the skin with salt and ground black pepper.

- Heat the olive oil in a large frying pan over medium heat. Add the chicken in batches, skin side down, and fry for 3 minutes, or until golden. Transfer each batch to the slow cooker.

- Drain the fat from the frying pan. Add the wine to the pan and bring to the boil, using a wooden spoon to scrape up any stuck-on bits from the bottom of the pan. Add the lemon juice and cook for another 1–2 minutes, or until the liquid has reduced by half.

- Pour the juices from the pan over the chicken in the slow cooker. Cover and cook on low for 6 hours.

- Turn the slow cooker heat to high. Add the beans, then cover and cook for a further 1 hour.

- Stir the olives and parsley through. Divide the chicken and vegetables among serving plates. Scatter with extra parsley and serve with lemon wedges.

CHICKEN SAVOYARDE

preparation time 20 minutes
cooking time 3 hours 35 minutes
serves 6

1 large onion, finely chopped

2 bay leaves

125 ml (4 fl oz/½ cup) good-quality chicken stock

125 ml (4 fl oz/½ cup) white wine

6 chicken breast fillets, about 1.25 kg (2 lb 12 oz) in total

250 ml (9 fl oz/1 cup) cream, at room temperature

1 tablespoon chopped tarragon

1 tablespoon dijon mustard

1½ tablespoons plain (all-purpose) flour

30 g (1 oz) butter, softened

100 g (3½ oz/¾ cup) grated gruyère cheese

40 g (1½ oz/1⅓ cups) ready-made mini-toasts

35 g (1¼ oz/⅓ cup) grated parmesan

2 tablespoons chopped flat-leaf (Italian) parsley

green salad, to serve

crusty bread, to serve

- Combine the onion, bay leaves, stock and wine in a slow cooker. Place the chicken breasts on top in a single layer, then season with sea salt and freshly ground black pepper. Cover and cook on low for 3 hours.

- Remove the chicken from the slow cooker to a warm platter. Cover with foil and keep in a warm place while finishing the sauce.

- Turn the slow cooker setting to high. Remove the bay leaves and stir in the cream, tarragon and mustard. Mix the flour and butter together in a small bowl, working them into a smooth paste. Whisking constantly, add the flour mixture to the liquid in the slow cooker.

- Cover and cook for 30 minutes, or until the mixture has thickened, whisking often to prevent lumps forming.

- Stir in the gruyère and season to taste with sea salt and freshly ground black pepper. Return the chicken to the sauce and heat briefly.

- Finely chop the mini-toasts, then toss in a small bowl with the parmesan and parsley.

- Divide the chicken among serving plates and drizzle generously with the sauce. Sprinkle the parmesan and parsley crumbs over the chicken and serve with a green salad and crusty bread.

CHICKEN GALANTINE WRAPPED IN PROSCIUTTO

preparation time 30 minutes
cooking time 2¼ hours
serves 4

10 g (¼ oz) dried porcini mushrooms
1 large double boneless chicken
    breast fillet, with tenderloins,
    about 725 g (1 lb 9 oz)
6 thin prosciutto slices, about 90 g
    (3¼ oz) in total
1 large handful baby English spinach
    leaves, about 30 g (1 oz)
2 tablespoons capers, drained
grated rind of ½ lemon

50 g (1¾ oz) butter
2 French shallots, finely chopped
2 garlic cloves, finely chopped
175 g (6 oz) mixed mushrooms,
    such as shiitake and Swiss brown,
    thickly sliced
60 ml (2 fl oz/¼ cup) white wine
1 tablespoon cornflour (cornstarch)
60 ml (2 fl oz/¼ cup) cream
roasted vegetables, to serve

● Put the porcini in a small bowl, cover with 125 ml (4 fl oz/½ cup) hot water and leave to soak.

● Remove the skin from the chicken and trim off any fat. Spread the two joined breasts out side by side on a chopping board, flesh side up. Without cutting through the join completely, make slits across the flesh to open the breast out, to more evenly distribute the flesh. Cover the chicken with a sheet of plastic wrap and pound gently with a mallet or rolling pin until the opened-out breast measures about 24 x 18 cm (9½ x 7 inches).

● Lay the prosciutto slices on a board in a line next to and overlapping each other, creating a sheet to wrap the chicken in. Place the chicken fillet evenly over them, along the widest length.

• Drain the porcini, reserving the soaking liquid, and chop. Lay the spinach over the chicken; scatter over half the porcini, the capers and lemon rind. Season well with freshly ground black pepper. Fold over to enclose the chicken, from the 18 cm (7 inch) shorter end. Tie with kitchen string to secure the chicken and prosciutto.

• Melt half the butter in a large frying pan over high heat. Add the chicken roll and sear on all sides for 2–3 minutes, or until the prosciutto is golden brown. Put the chicken in the slow cooker.

• Melt the remaining butter in the frying pan. Sauté the shallots, garlic and sliced mushrooms for 2–3 minutes. Add the wine, remaining porcini and the reserved porcini liquid and bring briefly to the boil. Pour over the chicken.

• Cover and cook on high for 1 ¾ hours, or until the chicken and mushrooms are tender. Using tongs, remove the chicken roll to a warm side plate. Cut off the kitchen string, cover with foil and leave to rest in a warm place.

• Blend the cornflour with 1 tablespoon water until smooth; stir into the sauce with the cream. Cover and cook for a further 15 minutes, or until the sauce has thickened a little.

• Carve the chicken into 8 thick slices. Serve with the mushroom sauce and roasted vegetables.

CHICKEN MADEIRA WITH MUSHROOMS

preparation time 15 minutes
cooking time 6 hours 10 minutes
serves 6

2 tablespoons plain (all-purpose) flour
1 kg (2 lb 4 oz) skinless chicken thigh
   fillets, trimmed of fat, then halved
1 large leek, white part only, rinsed
   well and chopped, plus extra leek
   slivers, to garnish
2 teaspoons chopped rosemary
2 bay leaves
250 ml (9 fl oz/1 cup) good-quality
   chicken stock

125 ml (4 fl oz/½ cup) madeira
20 g (¾ oz) butter
250 g (9 oz) button mushrooms,
   halved, or quartered if large
125 ml (4 fl oz/½ cup) cream
1 small handful chopped flat-leaf
   (Italian) parsley
lemon rind slivers, to garnish
mashed potato, to serve (see page
   146)

● Place the flour in a flat dish and season well with freshly ground black
pepper. Add the chicken and toss well to coat, shaking off any excess.

● Place the chicken in a slow cooker. Add the leek, rosemary and bay leaves,
then pour in the stock and madeira. Gently mix together.
Cover and cook on low for 5 hours.

● Melt the butter in a large frying pan then add the mushrooms and cook
for 5–10 minutes, or until golden, stirring occasionally. Then remove from the
frying pan and add to the slow cooker, then stir in the cream. Cover and cook
for a further 1 hour, or until the sauce is thick. Stir the parsley through. Season
the sauce with sea salt and freshly ground black pepper to taste.

● Serve the chicken on a bed of mashed potato, drizzled with the sauce
and garnished with leek and lemon rind slivers.

CHICKEN COOKED IN WHITE WINE

preparation time 40 minutes
cooking time 6 hours
serves 4

40 g (1½ oz/½ cup) fresh
   breadcrumbs
4 garlic cloves, crushed
3 rosemary sprigs, leaves removed
   and chopped

1 teaspoon grated lemon zest
1.5 kg (3 lb 5 oz) chicken
200 ml (7 fl oz) chicken stock
200 ml (7 fl oz) white wine

• In a small bowl, combine the breadcrumbs, garlic, rosemary and lemon zest
to make the stuffing.

• Rinse the chicken inside and out and pat dry with paper towels. Loosely stuff
the body cavity of the chicken with the stuffing, then tie or skewer the legs
together to secure the stuffing inside the chicken.

• Put the stock and wine in a small saucepan and bring to the boil.
Remove from the heat.

• Put the chicken, breast side down, in the slow cooker
and pour over the stock and wine mixture.
Cook on low for 6 hours, or until the chicken
is tender and the juices run clear when the
thigh is pierced with a skewer.

• Carve the chicken into pieces and serve with
the steamed butter potatoes and green
vegetables, if desired.

CREAMY BEEF WITH CHERRY TOMATOES AND SUN-DRIED TOMATOES

preparation time 25 minutes
cooking time 6½ hours
serves 6

35 g (1¼ oz/¼ cup) plain (all-purpose) flour

2 teaspoons sea salt

½ teaspoon freshly ground black pepper

1 teaspoon sweet paprika

1.5 kg (3 lb 5 oz) beef chuck steak, trimmed of fat, then cut into 3 cm (1¼ inch) chunks

1½ tablespoons tomato paste (concentrated purée)

60 ml (2 fl oz/¼ cup) white wine

1 onion, finely chopped

2 garlic cloves, crushed

500 g (1 lb 2 oz) cherry tomatoes, halved

90 g (3¼ oz/½ cup) semi-dried (sun-blushed) tomatoes, chopped

250 g (9 oz/1 cup) sour cream

400 g (14 oz) fresh pappardelle

toasted pine nuts, for sprinkling

small basil leaves, to garnish

shaved parmesan, to serve

- Place the flour, salt, pepper and paprika in a large bowl. Add the beef and toss until evenly coated. Shake off any excess flour, then place the beef in a slow cooker.

- Mix the tomato paste with the wine, then add to the beef with the onion, garlic, cherry tomatoes and semi-dried tomatoes. Gently mix together. Clean the sides of the bowl with a damp cloth if necessary.

- Cover and cook on low for 5–6 hours, or until the beef is very tender.

- Stir in the sour cream, then cover and cook for another 30 minutes, or until heated through.

- Meanwhile, near serving time, add the pasta to a large pot of rapidly boiling salted water and cook according to the packet instructions until al dente. Drain well.

- Divide the pasta among serving bowls, then spoon the beef mixture over the top. Sprinkle with the pine nuts, scatter the basil leaves and parmesan over the top and serve.

Entertaining

BOEUF EN DAUBE

preparation time 30 minutes
cooking time 8 hours 25 minutes
serves 4–6

2 tablespoons olive oil
1 kg (2 lb 4 oz) beef chuck steak,
    cut into 3–4 cm (1¼–1½ inch)
    chunks
8 pickling onions, about 400 g (14 oz)
    in total, peeled and halved
150 g (5½ oz) bacon, cut into
    1.5 cm (⅝ inch) pieces
1 carrot, peeled and chopped
1 celery stalk, chopped into 1.5 cm
    (⅝ inch) lengths
2 garlic cloves, crushed
1½ tablespoons plain (all-purpose)
    flour
1 tablespoon tomato paste
    (concentrated purée)

125 ml (4 fl oz/½ cup) good-quality
    beef stock
300 ml (10½ fl oz) red wine
1 tablespoon chopped thyme
2 bay leaves
400 g (14 oz) short pasta, such as
    casarecce, trofie or pasta twists
1 small handful chopped flat-leaf
    (Italian) parsley
crusty bread, to serve

- Heat half the olive oil in a large heavy-based frying pan over high heat. Add one-third of the beef and fry for 5 minutes, or until golden, turning to brown all over. Transfer the beef to a slow cooker. Brown the remaining beef in two more batches, transferring each batch to the slow cooker.

- Heat the remaining oil in the pan over medium–high heat. Add the onions, bacon, carrot and celery and cook, stirring, for 5 minutes, or until the vegetables are golden. Add the garlic and cook, stirring, for a further minute.

- Stir in the flour and cook for 1 minute, or until smooth. Gradually add the tomato paste, stock, wine, thyme and bay leaves. Cook, stirring, for 3 minutes, or until the mixture boils and thickens. Pour the sauce over the beef in the slow cooker.

- Cover and cook on low for 8 hours, or until the beef is very tender.

- Meanwhile, near serving time, add the pasta to a large pot of rapidly boiling salted water and cook according to the packet instructions until al dente. Drain well.

- Divide the pasta among wide, shallow serving bowls and spoon the beef mixture over the top. Sprinkle with the parsley and serve with crusty bread.

BEEF WITH CREAMY GREEN PEPPERCORN SAUCE

preparation time 25 minutes
cooking time 2 hours 5 minutes
serves 4

1 small onion, finely chopped
1 small carrot, peeled and finely
    chopped
1 celery stalk, finely chopped
2 garlic cloves, finely chopped
750 g (1 lb 10 oz) piece of beef fillet,
    trimmed of excess fat
8 thin slices of pancetta or streaky
    bacon, about 135 g (5 oz) in total
2 teaspoons olive oil
80 ml (2½ fl oz/⅓ cup)

good-quality beef stock
80 ml (2½ fl oz/⅓ cup) red wine
30 g (1 oz) butter
1 tablespoon cornflour (cornstarch)
80 ml (2½ fl oz/⅓ cup) cream
55 g (2 oz) tinned green peppercorns,
    rinsed and drained
mashed potato, to serve (see
    page 146)
steamed green beans, to serve

- Put the onion, carrot, celery and garlic in a slow cooker.

- Season the beef all over with freshly ground black pepper. Lay the pancetta slices on a clean work surface in a line next to each other, creating a sheet in which to wrap the beef. Place the beef fillet across the pancetta and fold the slices over to enclose the beef. Tie at intervals with kitchen string to secure the beef and pancetta.

- Heat the olive oil in a large frying pan over high heat. Add the beef roll and fry for 5 minutes, or until the pancetta is golden brown, turning to brown all over. Place the beef in the slow cooker, nestled among the vegetables.

- Place the frying pan back over the heat. Add the stock, wine and butter and stir to melt the butter. Bring briefly to the boil, then pour over the beef in the slow cooker.

- Cover and cook on high for 1 ¾ hours, or until the beef is tender. Using tongs, remove the meat to a warm side plate. Remove the kitchen string, cover the beef with foil and leave to rest in a warm place while making the sauce.

- Blend the cornflour with 1 tablespoon of water until smooth, then stir into the sauce in the slow cooker. Stir in the cream and peppercorns. Cover and cook for a further 10 minutes, or until the sauce has thickened a little.

- Carve the meat into thick slices and arrange on serving plates. Spoon the peppercorn sauce over. Serve with creamy celeriac and potato mash and steamed green beans.

Entertaining

SAUERBRATEN

preparation time 20 minutes plus 1–2 days marinating
cooking time 8 hours 45 minutes
serves 8

1 small onion, halved, then sliced
6 cloves
3 bay leaves
1 teaspoon black peppercorns,
    lightly crushed
250 ml (9 fl oz/1 cup) red wine
125 ml (4 fl oz/½ cup) red wine
    vinegar
2.25 kg (5 lb) beef bolar blade,
    in one piece
2 tablespoons olive oil

35 g (1¼ oz/1/4 cup) plain
    (all-purpose) flour
125 ml (4 fl oz/½ cup) good-quality
    beef stock
6 gingersnap biscuits
2 tablespoons soft brown sugar
lightly sautéed shredded cabbage,
    to serve
glazed baby carrots, to serve

- Put the onion, cloves, bay leaves and peppercorns in a saucepan. Pour in the wine, vinegar and 250 ml (9 fl oz/1 cup) water. Bring to the boil over medium heat, then transfer to a large heatproof bowl and set aside to cool. Add the beef and turn to coat in the liquid. Cover and refrigerate for 1–2 days, turning the beef occasionally.

- Heat half the olive oil in a large deep frying pan over medium–high heat. Drain the beef, reserving the marinade. Fry the beef for 10 minutes, turning to brown all over. Transfer to a slow cooker.

- Heat the remaining oil in the pan. Add the flour and cook, stirring, for 2 minutes. Remove from the heat and slowly whisk in the stock and reserved marinade. Return to the heat and cook for 3 minutes, or until the sauce has thickened. Pour over the beef.

- Cover and cook on low for 8 hours, or until the beef is very tender.

- Add the biscuits and sugar to the sauce and cook for another 30 minutes, or until the biscuits are soft. Whisk to dissolve the biscuits, then season to taste with sea salt and freshly ground black pepper.

- Carve the beef and divide among serving plates. Drizzle generously with the sauce and serve with sautéed cabbage and glazed baby carrots.

Note *Sauerbraten is a typical German winter dish. The beef is marinated in red wine vinegar with vegetables and spices and then slow cooked. Ginger biscuits are added to the sauce for a sweet and spicy flavour.*

CATALAN BEEF STEW WITH CHOCOLATE SAUCE

preparation time 20 minutes

cooking time 8¼ hours

serves 6

75 g (2½ oz/½ cup) plain
(all-purpose) flour

1 kg (2 lb 4 oz) beef chuck steak
or stewing beef, cut into 2 cm
(¾ inch) chunks

80 ml (2½ fl oz/⅓ cup) olive oil

185 ml (6 fl oz/¾ cup) red wine

2 large onions, chopped

1 carrot, peeled and diced

1 celery stalk, diced

1 leek, white part only, rinsed well
and thickly sliced

4 garlic cloves, quartered

400 g (14 oz) tin chopped tomatoes

375 ml (13 fl oz/1½ cups)
good-quality beef stock

60 g (2¼ oz/½ cup) grated
good-quality dark chocolate

steamed rice, to serve

1 large handful chopped flat-leaf
(Italian) parsley

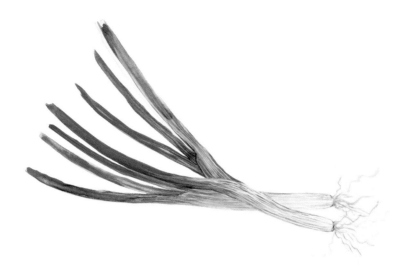

- Place the flour in a bowl and season with sea salt and freshly ground black pepper. Toss the beef in the flour to coat well, shaking off the excess.

- Heat half the olive oil in a large frying pan over medium–high heat. Add half the beef and fry for 2–3 minutes, or until golden, turning to brown all over. Transfer the beef to a slow cooker. Add the remaining oil to the pan and brown the remaining beef. Place in the slow cooker.

- Add the wine to the pan and cook, stirring, for 2 minutes, stirring with a wooden spoon to scrape up any stuck-on bits. Bring to the boil and allow to reduce by one-third. Remove from the heat and set aside.

- Place the vegetables, garlic and tomatoes in the slow cooker and toss gently to mix. Pour in the wine mixture and stock.

- Cover and cook on low for 7½ hours.

- Stir the chocolate through the stew. Cover and cook for a further 30 minutes. Season to taste with sea salt and freshly ground black pepper.

- Serve on a bed of steamed rice, sprinkled with the parsley.

SPANISH BEEF WITH CHORIZO

preparation time 10 minutes
cooking time 6 hours 20 minutes
serves 4

2 tablespoons extra virgin olive oil
1 kg (2 lb 4 oz) beef chuck steak,
    trimmed of fat and cut into 3 cm
    (1¼ inch) chunks
1 red onion, sliced
2 chorizo sausages, thickly sliced
2 garlic cloves, crushed
1 tablespoon smoked paprika
2 tablespoons tomato paste
    (concentrated purée)
2 x 400 g (14 oz) tins chopped
    tomatoes
1 red capsicum (pepper), trimmed,
    seeded and chopped into 3 cm
    (1¼ inch) chunks
sliced green chilli, to serve

BEAN AND ORANGE SALAD
400 g (14 oz) tin borlotti beans,
    rinsed and drained
1 small red onion, thinly sliced
1 small handful flat-leaf (Italian)
    parsley
finely grated rind of 1 orange
1 orange
2 tablespoons olive oil
1 tablespoon dijon mustard

- Heat the olive oil in a large heavy-based frying pan over medium–high heat. Add one-third of the beef and fry for 5 minutes, or until golden, turning to brown all over. Transfer the beef to a slow cooker. Brown the remaining beef in two more batches, transferring each batch to the slow cooker.

- Add the onion and chorizo to the pan and cook, stirring, for 2–3 minutes. Add the garlic, paprika and tomato paste and cook for 1 minute. Stir in the tomatoes and capsicum, stirring to scrape up any cooked-on bits. Transfer the mixture to the slow cooker.

- Cover and cook on high for 5–6 hours, or until the beef is very tender.

- To make the bean and orange salad, combine the beans, onion, parsley and orange rind in a large bowl. Peel the orange, removing all the white pith. Holding the orange over a bowl to catch any juices, cut along each side of the white membranes to remove the segments. Add the orange segments to the bean mixture. Whisk the olive oil and mustard into the reserved orange juice and season to taste with sea salt and freshly ground black pepper. Pour the dressing over the salad and gently toss together.

- Sprinkle the beef with the chilli. Serve with crusty bread and the bean and orange salad.

Note *Spanish paprika is called pimenton and is available in both a sweet and a smoked variety. Here we are using the smoked variety. Both varieties are available from spice shops and most supermarkets. If you have more time you can cook the beef on low, increasing the cooking time to 8–10 hours.*

Entertaining

NAVARIN OF LAMB

preparation time 25 minutes

cooking time 5 hours

serves 6

35 g (1¼ oz/¼ cup) plain (all-purpose)
flour
6 small French-trimmed lamb shanks,
about 1 kg (2 lb 4 oz) in total
2 tablespoons olive oil
1 onion, finely chopped
2 garlic cloves, crushed
250 ml (9 fl oz/1 cup) white wine
250 ml (9 fl oz/1 cup) good-quality
chicken stock

3 tablespoons tomato paste
(concentrated purée)
12 new potatoes, scrubbed
12 small baby turnips, peeled
12 small pickling onions, trimmed
and peeled
1 rosemary sprig
12 baby carrots, scrubbed
115 g (4 oz/¾ cup) frozen green peas,
thawed
mashed potato, to serve (see page
146)

- Spread 2 tablespoons of the flour on a plate and season with sea salt and freshly ground black pepper. Toss the lamb shanks in the flour to coat well; reserve the flour.

- Heat the olive oil in a large frying pan. Add the shanks and fry for 5 minutes, turning to brown all over. Transfer to a slow cooker, then sprinkle with any reserved flour.

- In a small bowl, mix together the onion, garlic, wine, stock and tomato paste, then pour over the shanks. Top with the potatoes, turnips, pickling onions and rosemary sprig. Cover and cook on high for 4 hours.

- Add the carrots, then cover and cook for a further 30 minutes, or until tender. Remove the shanks and vegetables to a warm platter. Cover with foil and keep in a warm place while finishing the sauce.

- Skim off any fat from the top of the sauce. Blend the remaining tablespoon of flour with 2 tablespoons water until smooth, then stir into the cooking liquid. Add the peas and cook for a further 10 minutes, or until the mixture has thickened slightly. Season to taste.

- Return the vegetables and lamb to the sauce to heat through. Serve on a bed of creamy mashed potato.

Note *If baby vegetables are not available, just use larger ones, cut to the appropriate size.*

SLOW-COOKED FENNEL AND ROSEMARY-SCENTED PORK BELLY

preparation time 20 minutes

cooking time 7 hours

serves 4

2 teaspoons fennel seeds, roughly crushed

2 teaspoons chopped rosemary

½–1 teaspoon chilli flakes

1 teaspoon sea salt flakes

½ teaspoon freshly ground black pepper

1 kg (2 lb 4 oz) pork belly, skin and rib bones removed

2 x 400 g (14 oz) tins butterbeans (lima beans), rinsed and drained

grated rind of 1 lemon

1 tablespoon lemon juice

1 tablespoon extra virgin olive oil

- On a large plate, mix together the fennel seeds, rosemary, chilli flakes, sea salt and pepper. Roll the pork belly over the spice mix to crust it with the spices.

- Place the pork belly in a slow cooker on a trivet, saucer or upturned cereal bowl.

- Cover and cook on low for 5–7 hours, or until the pork is very tender. The pork will have a slight pink blush inside when perfectly cooked.

- Remove the pork to a warm plate and cover with foil. Leave to rest in a warm place while finishing the sauce.

- Skim the cooking juices from the slow cooker and reserve about 80 ml (2½ fl oz/⅓ cup).

- Place the beans in a food processor with the lemon rind, lemon juice, olive oil and the reserved cooking juices, supplementing with a little stock or hot water if necessary. Purée for 4–5 minutes, or until smooth, scraping down the bowl with a spatula to mix well. Season to taste with sea salt and freshly ground black pepper.

- Heat the bean purée in a small saucepan, stirring regularly, or covered in a microwave oven. Serve the pork with the butterbean purée.

BRAISED PORK LOIN WITH CABBAGE AND POTATO

preparation time 30 minutes
cooking time 4¼ hours
serves 6

2 teaspoons fennel seeds

2 teaspoons caraway seeds

1 teaspoon sea salt

½ teaspoon paprika

1.2 kg (2 lb 10 oz) boned, rolled pork
 loin

1 tablespoon olive oil

1 bacon slice, cut into small dice

1 small onion, thinly sliced

1 tablespoon dijon mustard

60 ml (2 fl oz/¼ cup) white wine

60 ml (2 fl oz/¼ cup) good-quality

 chicken stock

1 tablespoon vinegar

125 ml (4 fl oz/½ cup) pouring cream

3 all-purpose potatoes, peeled

½ small red cabbage, finely shredded

- Using a mortar and pestle or spice grinder, crush the fennel seeds, caraway seeds, sea salt and paprika. Push three-quarters of the spice mixture inside the rolled pork, through the gaps at either end. Sprinkle the remaining spice mixture over the pork.

- Heat the olive oil in a non-stick frying pan over medium heat. Add the pork and brown on all sides (about 1 minute per side), and set aside.

- Add the bacon and onion to the pan and sauté for 3 minutes, or until softened. Add the mustard, wine, stock, vinegar and cream and stir to combine. Remove the pan from the heat.

- Thinly slice the potatoes using either a very sharp knife or a mandolin. Layer the potatoes in the base of the slow cooker and sprinkle each layer with salt. Next add the cabbage, top with the bacon and cream mixture, then add the pork.

- Cook on low for 4 hours, or until the pork is very tender.

- Remove the pork to a board and slice. Serve the pork with the potato and cabbage and top with the sauce.

BRAISED PORK WITH APPLES, APPLE CIDER VINEGAR AND CREAM

preparation time 15 minutes
cooking time 5 hours 20 minutes
serves 4

1 kg (2 lb 4 oz) pork shoulder or neck, rolled and tied with kitchen string
1 tablespoon olive oil
2 whole garlic cloves
2 tablespoons apple cider vinegar
125 ml (4 fl oz/½ cup) good-quality chicken stock

4 apples, peeled, cored and cut into wedges
125 ml (4 fl oz/½ cup) cream
1 tablespoon finely snipped chives
steamed green vegetables, to serve
toasted flaked almonds, to garnish (optional)

- Season the pork well with sea salt and freshly ground black pepper.

- Heat the olive oil in a heavy-based saucepan. Add the pork roll and fry for 8–10 minutes, or until deeply golden on all sides, turning often.

- Add the garlic to the pan, then pour in the vinegar and stock, stirring well with a wooden spoon to scrape up all the stuck-on bits from the bottom of the pan.

- Transfer the pork and pan juices to a slow cooker. Cover and cook on high for 4–5 hours, or until the pork is tender.

- Remove the pork to a warmed platter, cover with foil and leave to rest in a warm place while finishing the sauce.

- Strain the juices from the slow cooker through a fine sieve into a saucepan. Add the apples and cream and simmer, uncovered, for 5 minutes, or until the apples are tender.

- Remove the apples and keep warm.

- Simmer the sauce for another 5 minutes, or until it has reduced to the desired consistency.

- Remove the string from the pork, carve the pork into thick slices and arrange on serving plates. Top with apple wedges, drizzle with the sauce and sprinkle with the chives. Serve with steamed green vegetables, sprinkled with toasted flaked almonds if desired.

Entertaining

PORK NECK WITH STAR ANISE

preparation time 10 minutes
cooking time 8 hours 25 minutes
serves 6

1.5 kg (3 lb 5 oz) piece of pork neck
1 tablespoon olive oil
2 tablespoons soft brown sugar
2 bay leaves
1 cinnamon stick
4 cloves
2 star anise
500 ml (17 fl oz/2 cups) good-quality
    chicken stock
1 tablespoon cornflour (cornstarch)
mashed potato, to serve (see page
    146)

BRAISED RED CABBAGE
20 g (¾ oz) butter
1 tablespoon olive oil
1 granny smith apple, peeled,
    cored and thinly sliced
½ small red cabbage, finely shredded
60 ml (2 fl oz/¼ cup) apple juice
½ teaspoon caraway seeds (optional)

- Season the pork with sea salt and freshly ground black pepper.

- Heat the olive oil in a large frying pan over medium–high heat. Add the pork to the pan and cook, turning, for 10 minutes, or until browned all over. Transfer to a slow cooker. Sprinkle with the sugar, then add the bay leaves, cinnamon stick, cloves and star anise. Pour in the stock.

- Cover and cook on low for 8 hours, or until the pork is tender.

- Remove the pork to a warm platter. Cover with foil and keep in a warm place while finishing the sauce.

- Blend the cornflour with 1 tablespoon water until smooth. Add to the sauce in the slow cooker and stir in well. Cover and cook for a further 15 minutes, or until the sauce has thickened.

- Meanwhile, make the braised red cabbage. Heat the butter and olive oil in a large non-stick frying pan over medium heat. Add the apple and cook, turning often, for 3–4 minutes, or until light golden. Add the cabbage, apple juice and caraway seeds, if using. Cook, stirring, for another 5 minutes, or until the cabbage has just wilted. Season to taste.

- Carve the pork into thick slices. Serve with the braised red cabbage and mashed potato.

Note *The sauce can be thickened on the stovetop if it seems a bit runny. Blend 1 tablespoon cornflour (cornstarch) with 1 tablespoon of the pan juices and stir into the sauce. Bring to the boil, reduce the heat and simmer for 5 minutes, or until thickened.*

VEAL WITH TARRAGON LEMON CREAM AND BROAD BEANS

preparation time 25 minutes

cooking time 5¼ hours

serves 6

50 g (1¾ oz/⅓ cup) plain (all-purpose) flour

2 teaspoons sea salt

¼ teaspoon freshly ground black pepper

1.25 kg (2 lb 12 oz) veal stewing steak (blade or chuck), cut into 3 cm (1¼ inch) chunks

1½ tablespoons wholegrain mustard

125 ml (4 fl oz/½ cup) white wine

1 onion, very finely chopped

2 garlic cloves, crushed

2 tarragon sprigs, plus extra chopped leaves, to garnish

1 teaspoon grated lemon rind, plus extra strips, to garnish

60 ml (2 fl oz/¼ cup) cream

370 g (13 oz/2 cups) frozen or fresh broad (fava) beans, shelled

mashed potato, to serve (see page 146)

• Combine the flour, sea salt and pepper in a large bowl. Add the veal and toss until evenly coated, shaking off any excess flour. Transfer the veal to a slow cooker. Mix the mustard with the wine and add to the slow cooker along with the onion, garlic and tarragon sprigs. Gently mix together. Clean the sides of the cooker with a damp cloth if necessary. Cover and cook on low for 4 hours.

• Remove the tarragon sprigs and stir in the lemon rind and cream. Cover and cook for a further 1 hour, or until the veal is very tender. Stir in the broad beans and cook for a further 15 minutes to heat through.

• Ladle the veal into wide shallow serving bowls and generously spoon the sauce over. Garnish with extra lemon rind strips and chopped tarragon and serve with mashed potato.

PORTUGUESE SEAFOOD STEW

preparation time 20 minutes
cooking time 6½ hours
serves 4

¼ teaspoon saffron threads
1 leek, white part only, rinsed well
    and chopped into 1 cm (½ inch)
    pieces
1 chorizo sausage, halved and sliced
½ teaspoon smoked paprika
1 red capsicum (pepper), trimmed,
    seeded and chopped into 1.5 cm
    (⅝ inch) pieces
400 g (14 oz) tin chopped tomatoes

60 ml (2 fl oz/¼ cup) white wine
600 g (1 lb 5 oz) large raw king
    prawns (shrimp), peeled and
    deveined, leaving the tails intact
500 g (1 lb 2 oz) thick white fish
    fillets, chopped into 3–4 cm
    (1¼–1½ inch) chunks
2 tablespoons snipped chives
crusty bread, to serve
green salad, to serve

- Place the saffron in a small bowl, cover with 1 tablespoon very hot water and leave to infuse for 10 minutes.

- Put the leek, chorizo, paprika, capsicum, tomatoes and wine in a slow cooker. Add the saffron water and mix together well.

- Cover and cook on low for 6 hours.

- Add the prawns and fish, then cover and cook on high for a further 30 minutes, or until the prawns and fish are cooked through.

- Ladle the stew into wide shallow serving bowls and sprinkle with the chives. Serve with crusty bread and a green salad.

Entertaining

113

ZARZUELA

preparation time 40 minutes
cooking time 3½ hours
serves 6

250 ml (9 fl oz/1 cup) dry white wine
large pinch saffron threads
3 garlic cloves, thinly sliced
1 leek, white part only, thinly sliced
1 red capsicum (pepper), seeded and
    thinly sliced
1 green capsicum (pepper), seeded
    and thinly sliced
2 teaspoons paprika
400 g (14 oz) tinned chopped
    tomatoes
20 g (¾ oz) blanched almonds,
    finely chopped
1 bay leaf
1 small red chilli, seeded and chopped
60 ml (2 fl oz/¼ cup) brandy or
    cognac
2 tablespoons lemon juice
1.5 litres (52 fl oz/6 cups) good-
    quality fish or chicken stock

500 g (1 lb 2 oz) skinless firm white
    fish fillets, such as swordfish,
    monkfish or gemfish
500 g (1 lb 2 oz) small squid tubes
12 mussels
12 clams (vongole)
12 raw prawns (shrimp)
3 large flat-leaf (Italian) parsley sprigs

ROMESCO SAUCE

80 g (2¾ oz/½ cup) blanched
    almonds
285 g (10 oz) jar roasted red
    capsicums (peppers), drained and
    rinsed
2 teaspoons sweet paprika
2 slices stale white bread, torn into
    large pieces
2 garlic cloves, roughly chopped
2 tablespoons sherry vinegar
125 ml (4 fl oz/½ cup) extra virgin
    olive oil

- Combine the wine, saffron, garlic, leek, red and green capsicum, paprika, tomatoes, almonds, bay leaf, chilli, brandy, lemon juice and stock in the slow cooker. Cook on high for 3 hours.

- Meanwhile, prepare the seafood. Cut the fish into 2 cm (¾ inch) cubes. Clean the squid tubes and cut into rings. Scrub the mussels and clams with a stiff brush. Pull out the hairy beards from the mussels. Discard any broken mussels or clams or open ones that don't close when tapped on the work surface. Peel the prawns, leaving the tails intact. Gently pull out the dark vein from each prawn back, starting at the head end.

- Add the prepared seafood and parsley to the slow cooker and cook for a further 30 minutes, or until the seafood is cooked and the mussels and clams have opened. Discard any that remain closed. Remove the parsley from the soup.

- To make the romesco sauce, place the almonds, roasted capsicum, paprika, bread pieces, garlic and vinegar in the bowl of a food processor. Process until smooth, then gradually add enough of the olive oil until you have a thick sauce.

- Stir enough of the romesco sauce through the zarzuela to thicken it slightly. Divide among serving bowls and top with the remaining sauce. Serve with crusty bread.

Hot & spicy

Turn up the heat with this selection of bold and beautiful recipes from around the world.

GREEN CURRY OF TOFU AND VEGETABLES

preparation time 15 minutes

cooking time 6 hours

serves 4

300 g (10½ oz) orange sweet potato, peeled and cut into 1 cm (½ inch) dice

8 baby corn

3 tablespoons green curry paste

500 ml (17 fl oz/2 cups) coconut cream

300 g (10½ oz) firm tofu, cut into 3 cm (1¼ inch) chunks

2 zucchini (courgettes), thickly sliced

60 g (2¼ oz) green beans, trimmed and cut into 3 cm (1¼ inch) lengths

250 g (9 oz/1 bunch) broccolini, washed and halved lengthways

1–2 tablespoons fish sauce

400 g (14 oz/2 cups) jasmine rice

2 tablespoons lime juice

6 kaffir lime leaves, finely shredded

- Place the sweet potato and baby corn in a slow cooker. In a small bowl, whisk the curry paste and coconut cream until smooth, then pour over the vegetables.

- Cover and cook on high for 2 hours, or until the sweet potato is tender.

- Stir in the tofu, zucchini, beans, broccolini and 1 tablespoon of the fish sauce. Cover and cook for another 30 minutes, or until the green vegetables have softened.

- Meanwhile, near serving time, prepare the rice. Rinse the rice under cold running water until the water runs clear. Place the rice in a saucepan with 450 ml (16 fl oz) water. Bring to the boil and boil for 1 minute. Cover tightly, reduce the heat to as low as possible and cook for 10 minutes. Remove from the heat and leave to stand, covered, for 10 minutes.

- Stir lime juice and half the lime leaves through the curry. Check seasoning, adding another tablespoon of fish sauce if the curry needs more saltiness.

- Ladle the curry into wide shallow serving bowls. Garnish with the remaining lime leaves and serve with the rice.

Note *Kaffir lime leaves are available from greengrocers or Asian supermarkets. They are sometimes just labelled 'lime leaves', and can be frozen for later use. To finish the soup, you could stir some Thai basil through it and garnish with some extra Thai basil sprigs or leaves. Alternatively, garnish the curry with long green chilli halves.*

Hot & spicy

INDIAN-STYLE VEGETABLE CURRY

preparation time 15 minutes
cooking time 6½ hours
serves 4

1 onion, finely chopped
2 teaspoons finely grated fresh ginger
55 g (2 oz/¼ cup) mild curry paste (such as balti)
1 small handful curry leaves
375 ml (13 fl oz/1½ cups) good-quality vegetable stock
350 g (12 oz/2¾ cups) cauliflower florets
300 g (10½ oz) sweet potato, peeled and cut into 2 cm (¾ inch) chunks
1 zucchini (courgette), sliced

2 ripe tomatoes, chopped
60 g (2¼ oz/¼ cup) plain yoghurt
400 g (14 oz) tin brown lentils, rinsed and drained
45 g (1½ oz/1 cup) baby English spinach leaves
155 g (5½ oz/1 cup) frozen peas, thawed
3 tablespoons chopped coriander (cilantro) leaves
400 g (14 oz/2 cups) basmati rice

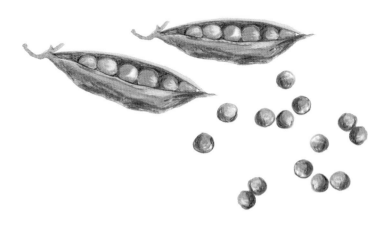

• Put the onion, ginger, curry paste, curry leaves and stock in a slow cooker. Add the cauliflower, sweet potato, zucchini and tomato and gently mix together.

• Cover and cook on low for 6 hours, or until the vegetables are tender.

• Stir in the yoghurt, lentils, spinach, peas and half the coriander. Cover and cook on high for a further 30 minutes, or until the spinach has wilted.

• Meanwhile, prepare the rice. Rinse the rice under cold running water until the water runs clear. Place the rice and 375 ml (13 fl oz/ 1½ cups) cold water in a large saucepan, then cover and cook over low heat for 20–25 minutes, or until the rice is tender.

• Spoon the rice into wide shallow bowls, then ladle the curry over the top. Sprinkle with the remaining coriander and serve.

Note *Curry leaves are highly aromatic and used extensively in Sri Lankan and southern Indian cooking, particularly in curries. They are available in Asian food stores and larger supermarkets.*

VIETNAMESE CARAMEL CHICKEN

preparation time 10 minutes
cooking time 5 hours 10 minutes
serves 4–6

1 kg (2 lb 4 oz) skinless, bone-in
   chicken thighs, flesh scored
2 lemongrass stems, bruised
400 g (14 oz/2 cups) jasmine rice
2 small carrots, peeled and cut into
   thin slivers, to garnish
3 spring onions (scallions), sliced on
   the diagonal
roasted peanuts, to garnish
baby basil leaves, to garnish

CARAMEL SAUCE
1 tablespoon peanut oil
2 teaspoons grated fresh ginger
2 garlic cloves, crushed
80 ml (2½ fl oz/⅓ cup) soy sauce
125 g (4½ oz/⅔ cup) dark brown
   sugar
60 ml (2 fl oz/¼ cup) fish sauce
60 ml (2 fl oz/¼ cup) Chinese rice
   wine

● To make the caramel sauce, heat the peanut oil in a small saucepan over medium heat; add the ginger and garlic and cook for 1 minute. Add the soy sauce and sugar and cook, stirring, for 3 minutes until the sugar has dissolved. Add the fish sauce and rice wine and reduce the heat to low. Simmer for 5 minutes, or until the sauce has thickened to a syrup consistency.

● Place the chicken in a slow cooker and pour the caramel sauce over the chicken. Turn to coat the chicken with the sauce. Add the lemongrass.

● Cover and cook on low for 5 hours, or until the chicken is tender.

● Meanwhile, near serving time, prepare the rice. Rinse the rice under cold running water until the water runs clear. Place the rice in a saucepan with 450 ml (16 fl oz) water. Bring to the boil and boil for 1 minute. Cover tightly, reduce the heat to as low as possible and cook for 10 minutes. Remove from the heat and leave to stand, covered, for 10 minutes.

● Spoon the rice into wide shallow bowls, then ladle the chicken mixture over the top. Garnish with the carrot, spring onion, peanuts and basil leaves and serve.

RED COOKED CHICKEN

preparation time 20 minutes
cooking time 6 hours
serves 6–8

2 x 1.2 kg (2 lb 10 oz) chickens,
   jointed
4 cm (1½ inch) piece of fresh ginger,
   peeled and sliced
115 g (4 oz/½ cup) soft brown sugar
1½ teaspoons fennel seeds
125 ml (4 fl oz/½ cup) hoisin sauce
250 ml (9 fl oz/1 cup) Chinese rice
   wine or medium–sweet sherry
250 ml (9 fl oz/1 cup) soy sauce
1 cinnamon stick

2 star anise
3 orange peel strips, each about
   2 cm (¾ inch) wide, white pith
   removed, plus thin orange rind
   strips, to garnish
500 ml (17 fl oz/2 cups) good-quality
   chicken stock
400 g (14 oz/2 cups) jasmine rice
2 spring onions (scallions), cut into
   long thin slivers
steamed bok choy (pak choy), to serve

• Put the chicken pieces in a slow cooker. In a small bowl, combine the ginger, sugar, fennel seeds, hoisin sauce, rice wine and soy sauce. Mix well to dissolve the sugar, then pour over the chicken pieces. Add the cinnamon stick, star anise and thick orange peel strips, then pour in the stock.

• Cover and cook on low for 5–6 hours.

• Meanwhile, near serving time, prepare the rice. Rinse the rice under cold running water until the water runs clear. Place the rice in a saucepan with 450 ml (16 fl oz) water. Bring to the boil and boil for 1 minute. Cover tightly, reduce the heat to as low as possible and cook for 10 minutes. Remove from the heat and leave to stand, covered, for 10 minutes.

• Remove the chicken from the slow cooker to a warmed platter, cover with foil and keep warm. Skim as much excess fat from the surface of the cooking liquid as possible. Discard the cinnamon stick, star anise and thick orange peel strips.

• Divide the chicken among wide shallow serving bowls, then ladle the broth over the top. Garnish with orange zest strips and spring onion slivers. Serve with the rice and steamed bok choy.

VIETNAMESE CHICKEN CURRY

preparation time 15 minutes
cooking time 6 hours
serves 6

1 kg (2 lb 4 oz) skinless chicken thigh
    fillets, trimmed and quartered
1 sweet potato, peeled and cut into
    2.5 cm (1 inch) chunks
1 tablespoon mild Indian curry
    powder
1 tablespoon caster (superfine) sugar
1 lemongrass stem, bruised
3 bay leaves
400 ml (14 fl oz) tin coconut milk
250 ml (9 fl oz/1 cup) good-quality
    chicken stock
400 g (14 oz/2 cups) jasmine rice
2 teaspoons fish sauce
lime wedges, to serve

CUCUMBER AND TOMATO SALAD

1 Lebanese (short) cucumber,
    seeded and sliced
12 cherry tomatoes, quartered
1 red chilli, thinly sliced
25 g (1 oz/¼ cup) bean sprouts,
    tails trimmed
1 small handful coriander (cilantro)
    leaves
1 teaspoon lime juice
¼ teaspoon sesame oil

• Put the chicken and sweet potato in a slow cooker. Sprinkle with the curry powder and sugar and gently mix them through. Add the lemongrass and bay leaves, then pour in the coconut milk and stock.

• Cover and cook on low for 6 hours.

• Meanwhile, near serving time, prepare the rice. Rinse the rice under cold running water until the water runs clear. Place the rice in a saucepan with 450 ml (16 fl oz) water. Bring to the boil and boil for 1 minute. Cover tightly, reduce the heat to as low as possible and cook for 10 minutes. Remove from the heat and leave to stand, covered, for 10 minutes.

• Meanwhile, make the cucumber and tomato salad. Combine all ingredients in a bowl and toss to combine.

• Stir the fish sauce through the curry. Season to taste with freshly ground black pepper.

• Spoon the rice into wide shallow bowls, then ladle the curry over the top. Serve with lime wedges and the cucumber and tomato salad.

Hot & spicy

CHICKEN TIKKA MASALA

preparation time 20 minutes plus at least 6 hours marinating
cooking time 8 hours
serves 6

1.5 kg (3 lb 5 oz) chicken thigh fillets, trimmed of fat
2 x 400 g (14 oz) tins chopped tomatoes
1 large onion, finely diced
½ teaspoon ground chilli
½ teaspoon ground ginger
125 ml (4 fl oz/½ cup) thick cream
steamed rice, to serve
1 large handful chopped coriander (cilantro) leaves
mango chutney, to serve

MARINADE

250 g (9 oz/1 cup) Greek yoghurt
2 tablespoons lemon juice
2 tablespoons tomato paste (concentrated purée)
5 garlic cloves, crushed
1 tablespoon grated fresh ginger
2 teaspoons ground cumin
2 teaspoons ground coriander
1 teaspoon garam masala
1 teaspoon ground turmeric
2 teaspoons sugar
1 teaspoon sea salt
½ teaspoon ground cardamom

MINT AND CHILLI RAITA

4 tablespoons mint
2 garlic cloves, crushed
1 long green chilli, seeded and finely chopped
1 teaspoon ground cumin
250 g (9 oz/1 cup) Greek yoghurt

• In a large bowl, mix together all the marinade ingredients. Add the chicken and toss to coat. Cover and refrigerate overnight, or for at least 6 hours.

• Place the tomatoes, onion, chilli and ginger in a slow cooker and mix together. Add the chicken and pour the marinade over the top.

• Cover and cook on low for 8 hours.

• Meanwhile, near serving time, make the mint and chilli raita. Place the mint, garlic, chilli, cumin and 1 tablespoon of the yoghurt in a food processor and blend until smooth. Add the remaining yoghurt and process until just combined. Season to taste with sea salt and freshly ground black pepper and transfer to a small serving bowl.

• Stir the cream through the curry. Serve the curry on a bed of rice, garnished with the coriander, with mango chutney and the mint and chilli raita to the side.

CHICKEN WITH HARISSA

preparation time 25 minutes
cooking time 7 hours 20 minutes
serves 4–6

2 kg (4 lb 8 oz) whole chicken
1 onion, peeled and halved
2 lemon zest strips
2 bay leaves
400 g (14 oz) tin chopped tomatoes
steamed couscous, to serve

HARISSA
1 red capsicum (pepper), trimmed,
   seeded and cut into quarters
1 teaspoon chilli flakes, or to taste
1 tablespoon ground cumin
3 garlic cloves, crushed
1 tablespoon extra virgin olive oil

- Start by making the harissa. Preheat the grill (broiler) to high. Place the capsicum on the grill tray, skin side up. Grill (broil) for 10 minutes, or until the skin blisters and blackens. Place the capsicum in a bowl and cover with plastic wrap. Leave to stand for 10 minutes, or until the capsicum is cool enough to handle. Peel the capsicum, discard the skin, then chop the flesh.

- Place the capsicum in a small food processor with the chilli flakes, cumin and garlic. Blend until finely chopped. Add the olive oil and process until almost smooth. Season the harissa to taste with sea salt and freshly ground black pepper.

- Wash the chicken and pat it dry with kitchen paper. Place half the onion, the lemon zest strips and bay leaves in the cavity of the chicken. Tie the legs together with kitchen string, then rub half the harissa over the chicken.

- Finely chop the remaining onion and place it in a slow cooker with the tomatoes and remaining harissa. Gently mix together, then rest the chicken on top.

- Cover and cook on low for 7 hours, or until the chicken is cooked through.

- Remove the chicken to a warm platter and cover with foil to keep warm.

- Transfer the sauce from the slow cooker to a small saucepan. Simmer over medium heat for 10 minutes, or until slightly reduced. Season to taste.

- Carve the chicken and serve on a bed of couscous, generously drizzled with the sauce from the slow cooker.

INDONESIAN BEEF STEW

preparation time 20 minutes
cooking time 4 hours
serves 6

1 kg (2 lb 4 oz) topside or rump
   beef steak
1 onion, chopped
2 carrots, peeled and coarsely grated
2 garlic cloves, finely chopped
375 ml (13 fl oz/1½ cups) good-
   quality beef stock
1 teaspoon sesame oil

2 tablespoons kecap manis
1 tablespoon light soy sauce
1 tablespoon tomato sauce (ketchup)
1 tablespoon sweet chilli sauce
400 g (14 oz/2 cups) basmati rice
fried Asian shallots, to serve
1 small handful coriander (cilantro)
   leaves, to garnish

• Trim the beef of excess fat, then cut into 4 cm (1½ inch) pieces.
Place in a slow cooker.

• In a bowl, mix together the onion, carrot, garlic, stock, sesame oil, kecap
manis, soy sauce, tomato sauce and sweet chilli sauce. Pour over the beef
and mix together well.

• Cover and cook on high for 4 hours, or until the beef is tender.

• Meanwhile, near serving time, prepare the rice. Rinse the rice under cold
running water until the water runs clear. Place the rice and 375 ml (13 fl oz/
1½ cups) cold water in a large saucepan, then cover and cook over low heat
for 20–25 minutes, or until the rice is tender.

• Ladle the stew into wide shallow serving bowls. Sprinkle with fried Asian
shallots and coriander and serve with the rice.

EGYPTIAN BEEF WITH OKRA

preparation time 15 minutes
cooking time 8 hours
serves 4–6

2 tablespoons plain (all-purpose) flour
1 tablespoon ground cumin
2 teaspoons ground coriander
800 g (1 lb 12 oz) beef chuck steak,
    cut into 3 cm (1¼ inch) chunks
2 onions, chopped
3 garlic cloves, crushed
70 g (2½ oz/¼ cup) tomato paste
    (concentrated purée)

400 g (14 oz) tin chopped tomatoes
12 okra, about 175 g (6 oz) in total,
    ends trimmed and chopped
400 g (14 oz/2 cups) basmati rice
125 g (4½ oz/½ cup) plain yoghurt
2 tablespoons pine nuts, toasted
1 large handful coriander (cilantro)
    sprigs

Hot & spicy

• Combine the flour, cumin and coriander in a large bowl. Add the steak and toss until evenly coated. Add the onion, garlic, tomato paste and tomatoes and mix well. Season with sea salt and freshly ground black pepper.

• Transfer the mixture to a slow cooker. Place the okra on top.

• Cover and cook on low for 8 hours.

• Meanwhile, near serving time, prepare the rice. Rinse the rice under cold running water until the water runs clear. Place the rice and 375 ml (13 fl oz/ 1½ cups) cold water in a large saucepan, then cover and cook over low heat for 20–25 minutes, or until the rice is tender.

• Check the seasoning of the stew and adjust if required. Spoon the rice onto serving plates, then ladle the beef over the top. Add a dollop of yoghurt, sprinkle with the pine nuts, garnish with coriander and serve.

VIETNAMESE BEEF BRISKET

preparation time 20 minutes
cooking time 7 hours
serves 4

1.5 kg (3 lb 5 oz) beef brisket, cut into
    3 cm (1¼ inch) chunks
2 carrots, peeled and thinly sliced
2 lemongrass stems, white part only,
    chopped
2 long red chillies, seeded and sliced
    on the diagonal
10 cm (4 inch) piece of fresh ginger,
    peeled and cut into thin
    matchsticks

60 ml (2 fl oz/¼ cup) soy sauce
2 tablespoons fish sauce
2 tablespoons lime juice
400 g (14 oz/2 cups) jasmine rice
quartered cherry tomatoes, to garnish
90 g (3¼ oz/1 cup) bean sprouts,
    tails trimmed
1 handful Vietnamese mint, to garnish
1 small handful small basil leaves,
    to garnish

- Place the beef, carrot, lemongrass, chilli, ginger, soy sauce and fish sauce in a slow cooker. Gently mix together.

- Cover and cook for 6 hours on low. Skim any fat from the surface of the sauce, then stir in the lime juice.

- Turn the slow cooker heat up to high, then cover and cook for a further 1 hour.

- Meanwhile, near serving time, prepare the rice. Rinse the rice under cold running water until the water runs clear. Place the rice in a saucepan with 450 ml (16 fl oz) water. Bring to the boil and boil for 1 minute. Cover tightly, reduce the heat to as low as possible and cook for 10 minutes. Remove from the heat and leave to stand, covered, for 10 minutes.

- Spoon the rice into wide shallow serving bowls, then ladle the beef mixture over the top. Garnish with the cherry tomatoes, bean sprouts, mint and basil and serve.

Note *This dish may also be served with rice noodles. Simply cover 300 g (11 oz) dried rice noodles with boiling water and allow to soak for 5 minutes, or until softened, then drain and rinse. Before serving with the beef brisket, stir some chopped coriander (cilantro) through the noodles if desired.*

CHINESE-STYLE BEEF WITH CUMIN

preparation time 15 minutes

cooking time 6 hours

serves 6

1.25 kg (2 lb 12 oz) beef chuck
steak, trimmed and cut into 4 cm
(1½ inch) chunks

1 tablespoon very finely sliced
fresh ginger

2 garlic cloves, crushed

1 tablespoon caster (superfine) sugar

2 teaspoons ground cumin

1 tablespoon chilli bean paste

125 ml (4 fl oz/½ cup) Chinese rice

wine

250 ml (9 fl oz/1 cup) good-quality
beef stock

60 ml (2 fl oz/¼ cup) light soy sauce

400 g (14 oz/2 cups) jasmine rice

1 teaspoon sesame oil

1 Lebanese (short) cucumber, seeded
and shredded

2 spring onions (scallions), cut into
thin slivers

1 small handful coriander (cilantro)
leaves

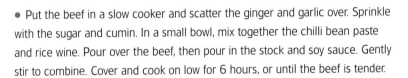

- Put the beef in a slow cooker and scatter the ginger and garlic over. Sprinkle
with the sugar and cumin. In a small bowl, mix together the chilli bean paste
and rice wine. Pour over the beef, then pour in the stock and soy sauce. Gently
stir to combine. Cover and cook on low for 6 hours, or until the beef is tender.

- Meanwhile, near serving time, prepare the rice. Rinse the rice under cold
running water until the water runs clear. Place the rice in a saucepan with
450 ml (16 fl oz) water. Bring to the boil and boil for 1 minute. Cover tightly,
reduce the heat to as low as possible and cook for 10 minutes. Remove from
the heat and leave to stand, covered, for 10 minutes.

- Stir the sesame oil into the beef mixture, then divide the beef among wide
shallow serving bowls. Ladle the cooking juices over the top. Garnish with the
cucumber, spring onion and coriander and serve with the rice.

INDIAN SPICED LEG OF LAMB

preparation time 30 minutes plus 1 day marinating

cooking time 7¾ hours

serves 4–6

1 onion, roughly chopped

4 garlic cloves

4 cm (1½ inch) piece fresh ginger, diced

2 tablespoons chopped coriander (cilantro) leaves

½ teaspoon ground cinnamon

½ teaspoon cardamom seeds

2 teaspoons ground cumin

½ teaspoon ground dried chillies

1 teaspoon ground turmeric

½ teaspoon garam masala

2 teaspoons curry powder

300 g (10½ oz) plain yoghurt

juice of ½ lemon

1.2 kg (2 lb 10 oz) lamb leg

2 egg yolks

● Put the onion, garlic, ginger and coriander in the bowl of a food processor and process until smooth. Add the cinnamon, cardamom seeds, cumin, chilli, turmeric, garam masala, curry powder and a pinch of salt. Process until combined. Stir in 200 g (7 oz) of the yoghurt and the lemon juice.

● Wash and dry the lamb. Cut slits in the side of the lamb, then coat the lamb in the yoghurt mixture, filling the slits. Cover with plastic wrap and place in the refrigerator to marinate for 24 hours.

● Put the lamb and the marinade in the slow cooker. Cook on low for 7 hours, or until the lamb is tender and cooked. Remove the lamb, cover and set aside.

● Combine the remaining yoghurt and the egg yolks. Stir into the liquid in the slow cooker and cook for 20–30 minutes, stirring occasionally, until the sauce has thickened slightly. Return the lamb to the slow cooker and cook for a further 10 minutes. Carve the lamb and serve with the sauce and steamed rice.

Hot & spicy

JAMAICAN LAMB WITH SWEET POTATO MASH

preparation time 20 minutes

cooking time 6 hours

serves 4

finely grated rind of 1 lime

60 ml (2 fl oz/¼ cup) lime juice

60 ml (2 fl oz/¼ cup) olive oil

3 garlic cloves, crushed

2 teaspoons ground cumin

1½ teaspoons cayenne pepper, or to taste

1 teaspoon ground allspice

1 teaspoon ground white pepper

1 teaspoon ground cinnamon

1 tablespoon thyme

1 kg (2 lb 4 oz) boneless, skinless lamb shoulder, cut into 4 cm (1½ inch) chunks

lime cheeks, to serve

SWEET POTATO MASH

900 g (2 lb) sweet potato, peeled and cut into 3 cm (1¼ inch) chunks

1 teaspoon ground cinnamon

40 g (1½ oz) butter

MANGO AND RED CHILLI SALSA

1 mango, finely diced

2 spring onions (scallions), finely chopped

1 small red chilli, finely chopped

- Put the lime rind, lime juice, olive oil, garlic, ground spices and thyme in a slow cooker. Add the lamb and gently mix until coated.

- Cover and cook on low for 5–6 hours, or until the lamb is tender, fragrant and has a little browning on top.

- Meanwhile, near serving time, make the sweet potato mash. Bring a saucepan of water to the boil, place the sweet potato in a steamer basket and set it over the saucepan. Steam the sweet potato for 10–15 minutes, or until tender. Place in a bowl, mash using a potato masher, then stir the cinnamon and butter through.

- Put all the mango and red chilli salsa ingredients in a small bowl and gently mix together. Set aside.

- Spoon the sweet potato mash into wide shallow serving bowls. Ladle the lamb mixture over the top. Serve with the mango and red chilli salsa, with lime cheeks for squeezing over.

TAMARIND LAMB

preparation time 20 minutes
cooking time 8¼ hours
serves 4

60 ml (2 fl oz/¼ cup) tamarind pulp
2 garlic cloves, crushed
1 tablespoon garam masala
1 teaspoon chilli flakes
1 teaspoon shrimp paste
1 teaspoon sugar
1 teaspoon freshly ground black
   pepper
½ teaspoon ground turmeric
2 tablespoons vegetable oil
1 kg (2 lb 4 oz) lamb shoulder, cut
   into 2 cm (¾ inch) chunks
2 large onions, roughly chopped
500 ml (17 fl oz/2 cups) good-quality
   chicken stock
coriander (cilantro) sprigs, to garnish
lime wedges, to serve

LEMON COUSCOUS
375 ml (13 fl oz/1½ cups) good-
   quality chicken stock
280 g (10 oz/1½ cups) instant
   couscous
40 g (1½ oz) butter
1 teaspoon finely grated lemon rind
1½ tablespoons lemon juice

- Put the tamarind pulp in a small bowl. Pour in 125 ml (4 fl oz/½ cup) hot water and mix well. Leave to soak for 5 minutes, then strain the mixture through a fine sieve into another small bowl, pressing on the solids with a spoon to extract all the pulp. Discard the solids.

- Stir the garlic, garam masala, chilli flakes, shrimp paste, sugar, pepper and turmeric into the tamarind water and set aside.

- Heat the oil in a frying pan over medium–high heat. Add the lamb in batches and fry for 2–3 minutes, or until brown on all sides. Transfer each batch to a slow cooker.

- Scatter the onion over the lamb, then pour in the tamarind water and stock.

- Cover and cook on low for 8 hours.

- Meanwhile, near serving time, prepare the lemon couscous. Bring the stock to the boil in a saucepan. Remove from the heat, add the butter and stir until melted. Place the couscous in a heatproof bowl with the lemon rind and lemon juice. Season well with sea salt and freshly ground black pepper and pour the stock over. Cover with a tea towel (dish towel) and leave to stand for 5 minutes, or until the liquid is absorbed. Fluff the grains up with a fork.

- Spoon lamb mixture into wide shallow serving bowls. Garnish with coriander sprigs and serve with the couscous and lime wedges.

LAMB SHANKS BRAISED WITH QUINCE PASTE

preparation time 30 minutes
cooking time 6½ hours
serves 6

1 onion, diced

2 garlic cloves, finely chopped

1 carrot, peeled and sliced

2 all-purpose potatoes, peeled and diced

90 g (3¼ oz/½ cup) dried apricots

180 g (6 oz/1 cup) pitted dates, halved

½ teaspoon mild paprika

½ teaspoon turmeric

½ teaspoon ground allspice

¼ teaspoon ground cardamom

100 g (3½ oz) quince paste, chopped

75 g (2½ oz/½ cup) plain (all-purpose) flour

6 French-trimmed lamb shanks

60 ml (2 fl oz/¼ cup) olive oil

80 ml (2½ fl oz/⅓ cup) red wine vinegar

1 litre (35 fl oz/4 cups) good-quality chicken stock

mashed potato, to serve (see page 146)

25 g (1 oz/¼ cup) toasted flaked almonds

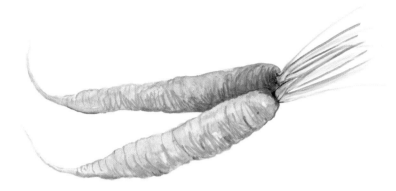

● Place the onion, garlic, carrot, potato, apricots, dates and ground spices in a slow cooker. Stir the quince paste through.

● Spread the flour on a large flat plate and season well with sea salt and freshly ground black pepper. Dust the shanks in the flour, shaking off the excess.

● Heat the olive oil in a large frying pan over medium–high heat. Add the shanks in batches and cook for 8 minutes, or until browned on all sides, turning occasionally. Remove each batch to the slow cooker, placing the shanks over the vegetables.

● Add the vinegar to the frying pan and cook for 1–2 minutes, stirring to scrape up any cooked-on bits. Pour the sauce over the lamb shanks, then pour in the stock.

● Cover and cook on low for 6 hours, or until the lamb is very tender and is falling away from the bone.

● Serve on a bed of mashed potato, topped with the flaked almonds.

YOGHURT-MARINATED LAMB WITH GARLIC AND SPICES

preparation time 25 minutes plus at least 8 hours marinating
cooking time 8¾ hours
serves 6

2.5 kg (5 lb 8 oz) leg of lamb leg,
    fat trimmed
2 onions, quartered
1 cinnamon stick
1 litre (35 fl oz/4 cups) good-quality
    chicken stock
2 tablespoons cornflour (cornstarch)
2½ tablespoons chopped mint
naan bread, to serve
lemon cheeks, to serve

YOGHURT MARINADE

2½ teaspoons cumin seeds
10 green cardamom pods, seeds
    extracted
5 garlic cloves, chopped
finely grated rind of 1 lemon
2½ tablespoons lemon juice
1 teaspoon ground turmeric
½ teaspoon chilli flakes, or to taste
500 g (1 lb 2 oz/2 cups) Greek
    yoghurt
2 teaspoons freshly ground black
    pepper

- Start by making the yoghurt marinade. Heat a small, heavy-based frying pan over low heat, add the cumin seeds and toast them without any oil, shaking the pan often, for 3–4 minutes, or until fragrant. Transfer to a mortar and pestle or electric spice grinder. Add the cardamom seeds and coarsely crush together. Tip the spice mixture into a small food processor. Add the garlic, lemon rind, lemon juice, turmeric and chilli flakes and process until the garlic is very finely chopped and the mixture is well combined. Scrape the mixture into a container large enough to fit the lamb. Add the yoghurt and pepper and mix together.

- Using a small sharp knife, make deep incisions all over the lamb. Place the lamb in the container and turn to coat well in the yoghurt mixture. Cover the container with plastic wrap and refrigerate for at least 8 hours, or overnight.

- Scrape as much of the yoghurt mixture from the lamb as possible, reserving the yoghurt mixture in the refrigerator.

- Place the onion quarters in a slow cooker with the cinnamon stick. Place the lamb on top and pour in the stock. Season the lamb well with sea salt, then cover and cook on low for 6–8 hours, turning the lamb over halfway during cooking.

- Near serving time, bring the reserved yoghurt mixture to room temperature.

- Remove the lamb to a warmed platter; cover with foil and keep warm. Remove the onion using a slotted spoon and discard. Turn the slow cooker setting to high. Combine the cornflour with enough of the yoghurt mixture to make a smooth paste, then stir into the remaining yoghurt mixture. Whisk the yoghurt mixture into the liquid in the slow cooker. Cover and cook for 30–40 minutes, or until the liquid has thickened, whisking often to prevent lumps forming. Stir in the mint.

- Tear the lamb into chunks. Serve drizzled with the yoghurt sauce, with naan bread, lemon cheeks and a salad.

Hot & spicy

CHILLI AND ANCHOVY LAMB NECK

preparation time 25 minutes
cooking time 6 hours
serves 4

1 onion, finely chopped
1 celery stalk, finely chopped
1 carrot, peeled and finely chopped
4 anchovy fillets, finely chopped
2 garlic cloves, finely chopped
1 large red chilli, chopped
2 kg (4 lb 8 oz) lamb neck chops,
    trimmed of excess fat and sinew
400 g (14 oz) tin chopped tomatoes
250 ml (9 fl oz/1 cup) good-quality
    chicken stock
125 ml (4 fl oz/½ cup) red wine
2 tablespoons finely chopped flat-leaf
    (Italian) parsley
steamed green beans, to serve

MASHED POTATO
800 g (1 lb 12 oz) spunta, sebago or
    coliban potatoes
40 g (1½ oz) butter, chopped
80 ml (2½ fl oz/⅓ cup) hot milk

GREMOLATA
1 handful flat-leaf (Italian) parsley,
    finely chopped
finely grated rind of 1 orange
1 small red chilli, seeded and finely
    chopped

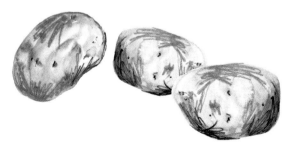

• Put half the onion, celery and carrot in a slow cooker.

• In a small bowl, mix together the anchovy, garlic and chilli. Spread the mixture over both sides of the lamb chops. Season well with freshly ground black pepper.

• Arrange the lamb chops in the slow cooker in a single layer. Scatter the rest of the vegetables over the top. Pour in the tomatoes, stock and wine.

• Cover and cook on high for 6 hours, or until the lamb is tender.

• Meanwhile, near serving time, make the mashed potato. Cook the potatoes in a large saucepan of boiling salted water for 20 minutes, or until very tender but not falling apart. Drain well, then return to the saucepan over low heat. Shake the pan gently until any remaining water evaporates. Using a potato masher, roughly mash the potatoes. Add the butter and hot milk and beat with a wooden spoon until fluffy. Season with sea salt and freshly ground black pepper.

• Mix together the gremolata ingredients and set aside until needed.

• Use tongs to remove the bones from the lamb chops if you wish. Divide the chops among serving plates and drizzle with the sauce from the slow cooker. Sprinkle with the gremolata and serve with the mashed potato and steamed green beans.

LAMB WITH GREEN OLIVES AND PRESERVED LEMON

preparation time 30 minutes
cooking time 3 hours
serves 4

½ preserved lemon
1 kg (2 lb 4 oz) lamb forequarter
  chops
1 onion, sliced
2 garlic cloves, crushed
2 cm (¾ inch) piece fresh ginger,
  finely diced
1 teaspoon ground cumin
½ teaspoon ground turmeric

130 g (4½ oz/¾ cup) green olives
625 ml (21 fl oz/2½ cups) chicken
  stock
400 g (14 oz) all-purpose potatoes,
  cut into 2 cm (¾ inch) dice
2 tablespoons chopped flat-leaf
  (Italian) parsley
2 tablespoons chopped coriander
  (cilantro) leaves

● Rinse the preserved lemon well, remove and discard the pulp and membrane and finely dice the rind.

● Trim the lamb of any excess fat and cut each chop in half.

● Put the lemon, lamb chops, onion, garlic, ginger, cumin, turmeric, olives and stock in the slow cooker. Cook on high for 2 hours. Add the potato and half the combined parsley and coriander leaves and cook for a further 1 hour, or until the lamb is tender and the potato is cooked.

● Stir through the remaining parsley and coriander and season to taste with salt and freshly ground black pepper. Serve with rice.

LAMB MADRAS

preparation time 25 minutes
cooking time 4 hours
serves 4

1 kg (2 lb 4 oz) boneless lamb leg
   or shoulder
60 g (2¼ oz/¼ cup) madras curry
   paste
1 onion, finely chopped
6 cardamom pods
4 cloves

2 bay leaves
1 cinnamon stick
185 g (6½ oz/¾ cup) Greek-style
   yoghurt
¼ teaspoon garam masala
2 long red chillies, chopped (optional)

• Trim the lamb of excess fat and cut into 3 cm (1¼ inch) cubes. Combine the curry paste and lamb in a large bowl and stir thoroughly to coat. Cover and marinate for at least 2 hours, or overnight, in the refrigerator.

• Put the marinated lamb, onion, cardamom pods, cloves, bay leaves, cinnamon stick and yoghurt in the slow cooker. Cook on high for 4 hours, or until the lamb is tender and cooked through. Season with salt and sprinkle with the garam masala. Garnish with chilli if desired and serve with rice.

Hot & spicy

MOJO PORK

preparation time 15 minutes
cooking time 8 hours
serves 6

1.5 kg (3 lb 5 oz) boneless pork loin,
    cut into 2 cm (¾ inch) chunks
2 teaspoons dried oregano
1 teaspoon chilli flakes
½ teaspoon freshly ground black
    pepper
2 tablespoons olive oil
1 large red onion, finely sliced
2 x 400 g (14 oz) tins chopped
    tomatoes
60 ml (2 fl oz/¼ cup) lime juice
60 ml (2 fl oz/¼ cup) orange juice
250 ml (9 fl oz/1 cup) good-quality
    chicken stock
1 small handful coriander (cilantro)
    leaves, to garnish

BEAN AND ORANGE SALAD
2 oranges, peel and white pith
    removed, cut into segments
300 g (10½ oz) tin butterbeans
    (lima beans), rinsed and drained
300 g (10½ oz) tin chickpeas, rinsed
    and drained
1 red onion, halved and finely sliced
1 small handful coriander (cilantro)
    leaves
2 tablespoons olive oil
2 tablespoons red wine vinegar
a pinch of caster (superfine) sugar

• Remove the rind and fat from the pork loin, then cut the meat into 2 cm
(¾ inch) chunks. Place the pork in a slow cooker and sprinkle with the oregano,
chilli flakes and pepper. Drizzle with the olive oil and gently mix to coat. Add the
onion and tomatoes, then pour in the lime juice, orange juice and stock.

• Cover and cook on low for 6–8 hours, or until the pork is tender.

• Meanwhile, just before serving, make the bean and orange salad.
In a salad bowl, toss together the orange segments, beans, chickpeas,
onion and coriander. Whisk together the olive oil, vinegar and sugar until
the sugar has dissolved. Season to taste with sea salt and freshly ground
black pepper, drizzle over the salad and gently toss.

• Ladle the pork mixture onto serving plates. Sprinkle with the coriander
and serve with the bean and orange salad.

THAI CHILLI BASIL PORK RIBS

preparation time 10 minutes plus overnight marinating
cooking time 10 hours
serves 4

250 ml (9 fl oz/1 cup) Thai sweet
　　chilli sauce
2 tablespoons tomato sauce (ketchup)
2 tablespoons dry sherry
2 tablespoons fish sauce
2 garlic cloves, crushed
2 teaspoons grated fresh ginger
1.5–2 kg (3 lb 5 oz–4 lb 8 oz)
　　American-style pork spare ribs

steamed rice, to serve
lime wedges, to serve (optional)

APPLE SALAD
1 green apple, cored and cut into
　　thick matchsticks
1 small handful coriander (cilantro)
　　leaves
1 green chilli, seeded and sliced
2 teaspoons lime juice

● In a large bowl, mix together the sweet chilli sauce, tomato sauce, sherry, fish sauce, garlic and ginger.

● Cut the ribs into segments of two or three ribs per piece. Add them to the sweet chilli mixture and toss well to coat. Cover with plastic wrap and refrigerate overnight.

● Transfer the ribs to a slow cooker. Pour the marinade mixture over the top. Cover and cook on low for 8–10 hours, turning the ribs occasionally during cooking and basting them with the sauce.

● Meanwhile, near serving time, make the apple salad. Place the ingredients in a small salad bowl and gently mix together.

● Divide the ribs among serving plates and drizzle with the sauce from the slow cooker. Serve with the apple salad, steamed rice and lime wedges, if desired.

FIVE-SPICE CARAMEL PORK

preparation time 20 minutes
cooking time 6¼ hours
serves 6

1.3 kg (3 lb) pork belly rind, skin
  removed
1 tablespoon vegetable oil
55 g (2 oz/¼ cup) caster (superfine)
  sugar
1 teaspoon Chinese five-spice
1 star anise
250 ml (9 fl oz/1 cup) good-quality
  chicken stock
1 tablespoon fish sauce
185 ml (6 fl oz/¾ cup) light soy sauce
steamed white rice, to serve

sliced red chilli, to serve (optional)

CUCUMBER AND GINGER SALAD
1 Lebanese (short) cucumber, shaved
  lengthways into thin ribbons
1 spring onion (scallion), finely sliced
  on the diagonal
1 cm (½ inch) piece of fresh ginger,
  peeled and cut into thin
  matchsticks
1 tablespoon peanut oil
2 teaspoons rice vinegar

Hot & spicy

● Cut the pork into 5 cm (2 inch) cubes. Heat the oil in a large frying pan over medium–high heat. Add one-third of the pork and fry for 5 minutes, or until golden, turning to brown all over. Transfer the pork to a slow cooker. Brown the remaining pork in two more batches, transferring each batch to the slow cooker.

● Sprinkle the pork with the sugar and five-spice and gently mix to coat. Add the star anise, then pour in the stock, fish sauce and soy sauce. Cover and cook on low for 6 hours, or until the pork is tender.

● To make the cucumber and ginger salad, combine the cucumber, spring onion and ginger in a salad bowl. Whisk together the peanut oil and vinegar, pour over the salad and gently toss together. Divide the pork among serving plates and drizzle with the cooking juices. Serve with steamed rice and the cucumber and ginger salad, sprinkled with sliced chilli if desired.

PULLED PORK

preparation time 20 minutes
cooking time 8¾ hours
serves 6–8

3 kg (6 lb 12 oz) piece of pork leg
    roast
1 large onion, very finely chopped
125 ml (4 fl oz/½ cup) tomato sauce
    (ketchup)
80 ml (2½ fl oz/⅓ cup) cider vinegar
55 g (2 oz/¼ cup) soft brown sugar
1½ tablespoons molasses
2 tablespoons tomato paste
    (concentrated purée)
2 tablespoons dijon mustard
1 tablespoon sweet paprika
1 teaspoon cayenne pepper
2 teaspoons cumin seeds
2 dried bay leaves
2½ teaspoons dried oregano
2½ tablespoons plain (all-purpose)
    flour
toasted bread slices, to serve
sliced gherkins (pickles), to serve

COLESLAW
60 g (2¼ oz/¼ cup) whole-egg
    mayonnaise
2 tablespoons lemon juice
125 g (4½ oz/1⅔ cups) finely
    shredded green cabbage
2 small carrots, peeled and roughly
    grated

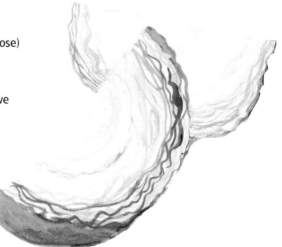

- Remove the skin and the layer of fat from the pork roast, then place the pork in a slow cooker.

- In a bowl, combine the onion, tomato sauce, vinegar, sugar, molasses, tomato paste, mustard, paprika, cayenne pepper and cumin seeds. Stir until smooth, then pour over the pork in the slow cooker. Add the bay leaves.

- Cover and cook on low for 8 hours, or until the pork is very tender.

- Remove the pork to a large plate or bowl and leave to cool slightly.

- Add the oregano to the slow cooker and turn the heat to high. In a small bowl, combine the flour with 250 ml (9 fl oz/1 cup) of the cooking liquid, whisking until smooth. Whisk the flour mixture into the liquid in the slow cooker. Cover and cook for 30–35 minutes, or until the sauce has thickened, whisking occasionally to prevent lumps forming.

- Meanwhile, make the coleslaw. Combine the mayonnaise and lemon juice in a large bowl and mix well. Add the cabbage and carrot and toss until well combined. Set aside.

- Shred the pork, using your hands. Add the shredded pork to the slow cooker, then cover and cook on high for a final 10 minutes, or until the pork is heated through.

- Serve the pulled pork on toasted bread, with the coleslaw and gherkins.

Hot & spicy

RED-COOKED PORK BELLY

preparation time 15 minutes
cooking time 7 hours
serves 6

1 kg (2 lb 4 oz) pork belly
500 ml (17 fl oz/2 cups) chicken stock
60 ml (2 fl oz/¼ cup) dark soy sauce
60 ml (2 fl oz/¼ cup) Chinese rice
   wine
6 dried shiitake mushrooms
4 garlic cloves, bruised
5 x 5 cm (2 x 2 inch) piece fresh
   ginger, sliced

1 piece dried mandarin or tangerine
   peel
2 teaspoons sichuan peppercorns
2 star anise
1 cinnamon stick
2 tablespoons Chinese rock sugar
1 teaspoon sesame oil
3 spring onions (scallions), thinly
   sliced diagonally

• Put the pork belly, stock, soy sauce, rice wine, mushrooms, garlic, ginger, mandarin peel, peppercorns, star anise, cinnamon stick, rock sugar and sesame oil in the slow cooker. Cook on low for 6 hours, or until the pork is very tender. Remove the pork from the stock and set aside.

• Strain the liquid into a bowl, set the mushrooms aside, then return the strained liquid to the slow cooker. Increase the heat to high and cook, uncovered, for a further 1 hour, or until the liquid has reduced and thickened. About 15 minutes before the end of cooking time, return the pork and mushrooms to the slow cooker to heat through.

• Remove the pork from the stock and cut into 1 cm (½ inch) thick slices. Transfer to a platter with the mushrooms and spoon over some of the cooking liquid. Sprinkle over the spring onions and serve with rice.

Note: Chinese rock sugar is a crystallised form of pure sugar. It imparts a rich flavour, especially to braised or 'red-cooked' foods, and gives them a translucent glaze.

MA PO TOFU WITH PORK

preparation time 20 minutes
cooking time 2½ hours
serves 4–6

2 tablespoons fermented black beans

400 g (14 oz) minced (ground) pork

1 tablespoon finely chopped fresh
   ginger

3 spring onions (scallions), finely
   chopped

125 ml (4 fl oz/½ cup) good-quality
   chicken stock

2 tablespoons soy sauce

1 tablespoon chilli bean paste

2 tablespoons Chinese rice wine

450 g (1 lb) firm tofu, cut into 1.5 cm
   (⅝ inch) cubes

2 garlic cloves, chopped

1 tablespoon cornflour (cornstarch)

2 teaspoons sesame oil

spring onions (scallions), extra, sliced
   diagonally, to serve

• Put the black beans in a bowl of cold water and soak for 5 minutes.
Drain and finely chop.

• Put the beans, pork, ginger, spring onion, stock, soy sauce, chilli bean paste
and rice wine in the slow cooker. Cook on low for 2 hours.

• Add the tofu and garlic and stir gently until the tofu is well coated with the
sauce. Cook for a further 20–30 minutes, or until the mixture has thickened.
Garnish with the extra spring onions and serve with rice.

Hot & spicy

157

PORK AND LEMONGRASS CURRY

preparation time 15 minutes
cooking time 6 hours 20 minutes
serves 4

1 tablespoon peanut oil
1 kg (2 lb 4 oz) pork shoulder, cut into
   2 cm (¾ inch) chunks
270 ml (9½ fl oz) tin coconut cream
400 g (14 oz/2 cups) jasmine rice
40 g (1½ oz/¼ cup) roasted peanuts,
   chopped, to garnish
1 small handful chopped mint,
   to garnish
1 long red chilli, thinly sliced,
   to garnish
lime wedges, to serve

LEMONGRASS CURRY PASTE

1 onion, chopped
2 garlic cloves, chopped
2 small bird's eye chillies, chopped
2 red Asian shallots, peeled and
   chopped
3 tablespoons chopped lemongrass,
   white part only
1 handful coriander (cilantro) leaves,
   chopped
2 tablespoons Thai green curry paste

- To make the lemongrass curry paste, place the onion, garlic, chilli, shallots, lemongrass, coriander, curry paste and 2 tablespoons water in a food processor and process to form a smooth paste. Set aside.

- Heat the peanut oil in a large frying pan over medium heat. Add the pork in batches and fry for 5 minutes, turning to brown all over and transferring each batch to a slow cooker.

- Add any pan juices from the pork to the slow cooker. Stir in the lemongrass curry paste, then pour in the coconut cream.

- Cover and cook on low for 6 hours.

- Meanwhile, near serving time, prepare the rice. Rinse the rice under cold running water until the water runs clear. Place the rice in a saucepan with 450 ml (16 fl oz) water. Bring to the boil and boil for 1 minute. Cover tightly, reduce the heat to as low as possible and cook for 10 minutes. Remove from the heat and leave to stand, covered, for 10 minutes.

- Spoon the rice into wide shallow bowls, then ladle the pork mixture over the top. Sprinkle with the peanuts, mint and chilli and serve with lime wedges.

MOROCCAN FISH TAGINE

preparation time 20 minutes
cooking time 3½ hours
serves 4

1 red onion, sliced
8 new potatoes, cut in half
4 roma (plum) tomatoes, quartered
6 garlic cloves
1 red capsicum (pepper), trimmed,
    seeded and sliced
100 g (3½ oz) pitted black olives
125 ml (4 fl oz/½ cup) good-quality
    fish stock
a pinch of saffron threads
4 x 200 g (7 oz) firm white skinless
    fish fillets (such as ling)
2 tablespoons chopped preserved

lemon rind
flat-leaf (Italian) parsley, to garnish
steamed couscous, to serve

CHERMOULA

1 tablespoon olive oil
2 garlic cloves, crushed
1 large handful coriander (cilantro)
    leaves, chopped
2 teaspoons ground cumin
2 teaspoons ground paprika
60 ml (2 fl oz/¼ cup) lemon juice
1 teaspoon sea salt

• Place onion, potato, tomatoes, garlic, capsicum and olives in a slow cooker.
Put all the chermoula ingredients in a food processor and blend until a smooth
paste forms. Mix 1 tablespoon of the chermoula into the stock until smooth,
reserving the remainder for rubbing over the fish. Stir saffron threads into the
stock, then pour over the vegetables in the slow cooker. Mix well to combine.
Cover and cook on high for 3 hours, or until the potatoes are tender.

• About 15 minutes before the vegetables are cooked, spread the remaining
chermoula over both sides of each fish fillet and set aside for the flavours to be
absorbed. Add the fish to the slow cooker, then cover and cook for a further
30 minutes, or until the fish flakes when tested with a fork. Stir the preserved
lemon through the tagine. Garnish with parsley and serve with couscous.

SRI LANKAN FISH CURRY

preparation time 15 minutes
cooking time 3 hours
serves 6

1 onion, cut into wedges
2 long green chillies, halved
   lengthways, then seeded and
   chopped
2 garlic cloves, finely chopped
1 tablespoon Indian curry powder
2 cm (¾ inch) piece of fresh ginger,
   peeled and cut into thin
   matchsticks
1 cinnamon stick
1 small handful curry leaves
2 teaspoons tamarind purée

400 ml (14 fl oz) tin coconut milk
125 ml (4 fl oz/½ cup) good-quality
   chicken or fish stock
900 g (2 lb) firm white fish fillets,
   such as ling
2 tablespoons lime juice
steamed rice, to serve
2 tomatoes, seeded and finely
   chopped, to garnish
coriander (cilantro) leaves, to garnish
lime wedges, to serve

Hot & spicy

● Put the onion, chilli, garlic, curry powder, ginger, cinnamon stick and curry
leaves in a slow cooker. Drizzle the tamarind purée over the top. Pour in the
coconut milk and stock and mix together. Add the fish and gently mix to coat.

● Cover and cook on low for 3 hours.

● Stir the lime juice through the curry and season well with sea salt and freshly
ground black pepper.

● Serve on a bed of steamed rice, garnished with chopped tomato and
coriander leaves, with lime wedges for squeezing over.

Pulses & grains

Packed with flavour, pulses and grains are made for the slow-cooking process. They're a source of valuable nutrients, too.

POLENTA AND VEGETABLE HOTPOT

preparation time 20 minutes
cooking time 2–3 hours
serves 4–6

2 tablespoons olive oil
300 g (10½ oz/2 cups) polenta
¼ teaspoon paprika
pinch cayenne pepper
1.5 litres (52 fl oz/6 cups) vegetable
   stock or water
3 spring onions (scallions), chopped
1 large tomato, chopped
1 zucchini (courgette), chopped
1 red or green capsicum (pepper),
   seeded and chopped
300 g (10½ oz) pumpkin (winter
   squash), peeled and cut into
    1.5 cm (⅝ inch) dice

100 g (3½ oz) button mushrooms,
   chopped
300 g (10½ oz) tinned corn kernels,
   drained
100 g (3½ oz/1 cup) freshly grated
   parmesan cheese
1 handful flat-leaf (Italian) parsley,
   chopped
125 ml (4 fl oz/½ cup) pouring cream
   (optional)

- Pour 1 tablespoon of the olive oil into the slow cooker bowl and spread it over the base and side. Pour in the polenta, then add the paprika, cayenne pepper, 1 teaspoon salt and some freshly ground black pepper. Stir in the stock and remaining oil. Stir to combine.

- Add the spring onion, tomato, zucchini, capsicum, pumpkin, mushrooms and corn and mix well. Cook on high for 2–3 hours, or until the polenta is soft and the vegetables are cooked. Stir several times with a fork to keep the polenta from setting on the base. Start checking after 2 hours to see if the vegetables are tender.

- Before serving, stir through the parmesan and parsley. For a richer taste, stir through the cream. Taste and season with extra salt and freshly ground black pepper if necessary. Serve with a green salad.

note *You can also serve this vegetable hotpot as an accompaniment to barbecued meats.*

OSSO BUCO WITH POLENTA

preparation time 25 minutes
cooking time 8½ hours
serves 4–6

35 g (1¼ oz/¼ cup) plain (all-purpose)
   flour
8 beef osso buco, about 1.5 kg
   (3 lb 5 oz) in total
2 tablespoons olive oil
1 onion, finely chopped
1 celery stalk, finely chopped
1 carrot, peeled and finely chopped
400 g (14 oz) tin chopped tomatoes
2 bay leaves
2 rosemary sprigs
375 ml (13 fl oz/1½ cups)
   good-quality chicken stock

185 ml (6 fl oz/¾ cup) white wine
100 g (3½ oz/½ cup) green olives
3 tablespoons chopped flat-leaf
   (Italian) parsley, plus extra,
   to garnish

SOFT POLENTA
500 ml (17 fl oz/2 cups) milk
150 g (5½ oz/1 cup) white or yellow
   polenta
40 g (1½ oz) butter
35 g (1¼ oz/⅓ cup) grated parmesan

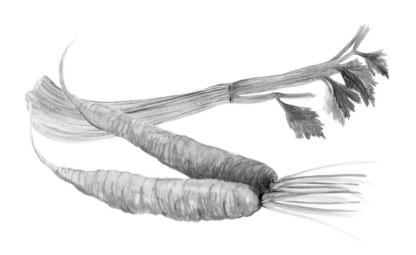

• Put the flour in a flat dish and season with sea salt and freshly ground black pepper. Dust the osso buco in the seasoned flour.

• Heat the olive oil in a large frying pan over medium–high heat. Add the osso buco in batches and cook for 5 minutes on each side, or until golden brown all over, transferring each batch to a slow cooker.

• Add the onion, celery, carrot, tomatoes, bay leaves and rosemary sprigs to the slow cooker, then pour in the stock and wine.

• Cover and cook on low for 8 hours, or until the meat is very tender.

• Meanwhile, near serving time, make the soft polenta. Put the milk in a saucepan with 250 ml (9 fl oz/1 cup) water and bring to the boil. Stirring continuously, add the polenta in a thin, steady stream. Cook over low heat, stirring often, for 30–35 minutes, or until the polenta is thick and soft. Remove from the heat and stir in the butter and parmesan.

• Stir the olives and parsley through the osso buco mixture. Season to taste with sea salt and freshly ground black pepper.

• Serve the osso buco on a bed of soft polenta, sprinkled with extra parsley.

Pulses & grains

AFRICAN CHICKEN WITH COUSCOUS

preparation time 20 minutes
cooking time 6½ hours
serves 4

1 tablespoon olive oil
4 chicken drumsticks
4 chicken wings, wing tips removed
    and cut into two pieces at the joint
2 chicken thigh cutlets, quartered
2 onions, finely sliced
2 tablespoons berbere spice blend
2 garlic cloves, crushed
60 g (2¼ oz/¼ cup) tomato paste
    (concentrated purée)
400 g (14 oz) tin chopped tomatoes
coriander (cilantro) sprigs, to garnish
lemon cheeks, to serve

HERBED COUSCOUS
280 g (10 oz/1½ cups) instant
    couscous
1 small handful coriander (cilantro)
    leaves, chopped
1 tablespoon olive oil

- Heat the olive oil in a large frying pan over medium–high heat. Brown the chicken pieces in batches for 5 minutes, or until golden all over, turning during cooking. Transfer each batch to a slow cooker.

- Add the onion to the frying pan and cook, stirring occasionally, for 10 minutes, or until softened. Spread the onion over the chicken pieces in the slow cooker.

- Add the berbere spice blend to the frying pan and cook for 1 minute, or until fragrant. Stir in the garlic and tomato paste and cook for 30 seconds. Add the tomatoes and cook, stirring, for 1 minute, or until heated through. Transfer the mixture to the slow cooker and gently mix through.

- Cover and cook on high for 5–6 hours, or until the chicken is very tender. Season with sea salt to taste.

- Meanwhile, near serving time, make the herbed couscous. Place the couscous in a heatproof bowl and pour in 375 ml (13 fl oz/1 ½ cups) boiling water. Cover with a tea towel (dish towel) and leave to stand for 5 minutes, or until the liquid is absorbed. Fluff the grains up with a fork, then stir in the coriander and olive oil. Season to taste with sea salt and freshly ground black pepper.

- Spoon the couscous into wide shallow serving bowls. Arrange the chicken pieces over the top and drizzle with the sauce from the slow cooker. Garnish with coriander and serve with lemon cheeks.

Note Berbere is an African spice blend of salt, ground cumin, ground coriander, ground pepper, ajowan, fenugreek, allspice, ginger, chilli, nutmeg and cloves. You can buy it at specialty spice shops, but if you can't find it, use a Moroccan spice mix from the supermarket.

Pulses & grains

CHICKEN AND LENTIL CURRY

preparation time 25 minutes plus 3 hours marinating
cooking time 4 hours 10 minutes
serves 4

10 skinless chicken thigh fillets,
   about 1 kg (2 lb 4 oz) in total
2 tablespoons Indian curry paste,
   such as madras
2 garlic cloves, finely chopped
2 teaspoons grated fresh ginger
1 long red chilli, seeded and finely
   chopped
8 spring onions (scallions), sliced on
   the diagonal
1 green capsicum (pepper), trimmed,
   seeded and sliced

350 g (12 oz) purple sweet potato,
   peeled and sliced on the diagonal
   into 3 cm (1¼ inch) chunks
400 g (14 oz) tin chopped tomatoes
125 ml (4 fl oz/½ cup) good-quality
   chicken stock
400 g (14 oz/2 cups) basmati rice
400 g (14 oz) tin green or brown
   lentils, rinsed and drained
coriander (cilantro) sprigs, to garnish
lime cheeks, to serve
Greek yoghurt, to serve

- Trim the chicken thighs of excess fat and cut them into quarters.

- In a large bowl, mix together the curry paste, garlic, ginger and chilli. Add the chicken and stir to thoroughly coat it in the spices. Cover and marinate in the refrigerator for 3 hours to develop the flavours.

- Add the spring onion, capsicum, sweet potato, tomatoes and stock to the chicken mixture. Gently toss together, then transfer to a slow cooker. Cover and cook on high for 4 hours, or until the chicken and sweet potato are tender.

- Meanwhile, near serving time, prepare the rice. Rinse the rice under cold running water until the water runs clear. Place the rice and 375 ml (13 fl oz/ 1½ cups) cold water in a large saucepan, then cover and cook over low heat for 20–25 minutes, or until the rice is tender.

- Meanwhile, add the lentils to the slow cooker and stir through the chicken mixture. Cover and cook for a further 10 minutes, or until the lentils are warmed through.

- Spoon the rice into wide shallow serving bowls, then ladle the curry over the top. Garnish with coriander sprigs. Serve with lime cheeks and a small bowl of yoghurt.

Pulses & grains

VEGETARIAN CHILLI BEANS

preparation time 10 minutes
cooking time 4 hours
serves 4

1 onion, chopped
1 red capsicum (pepper), trimmed,
   seeded and chopped
400 g (14 oz) tin chopped tomatoes
2 x 400 g (14 oz) tins red kidney
   beans, rinsed and drained
1 tablespoon tomato paste
   (concentrated purée)
3 teaspoons ground coriander
2 teaspoons ground cumin
½ teaspoon chilli powder
2 garlic cloves, crushed
2 bay leaves
125 ml (4 fl oz/½ cup) good-quality
   chicken stock

400 g (14 oz/2 cups) basmati rice
90 g (3¼ oz/⅓ cup) sour cream
1 small handful coriander (cilantro)
   sprigs
flour tortillas, to serve

AVOCADO SALSA
1 avocado, peeled and diced
2 tablespoons lemon juice
1 roma (plum) tomato, seeded and
   diced
½ red onion, thinly sliced

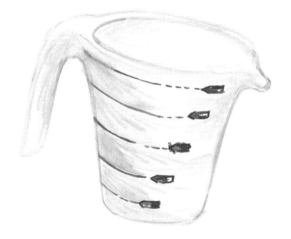

- Place the onion, capsicum, tomatoes, beans, tomato paste, coriander, cumin, chilli powder, garlic and bay leaves in a slow cooker. Pour in the stock and stir to combine well. Cover and cook for 4 hours on low.

- Meanwhile, near serving time, prepare the rice. Rinse the rice under cold running water until the water runs clear. Place the rice and 375 ml (13 fl oz/ 1½ cups) cold water in a large saucepan, then cover and cook over low heat for 20–25 minutes, or until the rice is tender.

- To make the avocado salsa, put all the ingredients in a bowl and stir to combine. Season to taste with sea salt and freshly ground black pepper. Cover and refrigerate until required.

- Spoon the chilli beans into serving bowls. Top with a dollop of the sour cream and garnish with the coriander sprigs. Serve with the rice, avocado salsa and tortillas.

MOROCCAN RATATOUILLE

preparation time 25 minutes
cooking time 4½ hours
serves 6

80 ml (2½ fl oz/⅓ cup) olive oil,
  approximately
2 large red onions, cut into 2 cm
  (¾ inch) chunks
2 eggplants (aubergine), about 450 g
  (1 lb) each, trimmed and cut into
  2.5 cm (1 inch) chunks
2 large red capsicums (peppers),
  trimmed, seeded and chopped into
  2.5 cm (1 inch) chunks
2 tablespoons Moroccan spice mix
2 x 400 g (14 oz) tins chopped
  tomatoes
2 tablespoons tomato paste
  (concentrated purée)

400 g (14 oz) tin chickpeas, rinsed
  and drained
750 g (1 lb 10 oz) butternut pumpkin
  (squash), peeled, seeded and cut
  into 3 cm (1¼ inch) chunks
2 tablespoons lemon juice
2½ teaspoons honey
110 g (33/4 oz/⅔ cup) pimento-
  stuffed green olives
2 tablespoons chopped coriander
  (cilantro)
250 g (9 oz/1 cup) Greek yoghurt
1 tablespoon chopped mint
steamed rice, to serve
harissa paste, to serve

- Heat 1 tablespoon of the olive oil in a large heavy-based frying pan over medium heat. Add the onion and cook, tossing occasionally, for 4 minutes, or until the onion starts to soften and brown. Transfer the onion to a slow cooker.

- Heat another 1 tablespoon of oil in the pan and add half the eggplant. Cook for 2 minutes on each side, or until the eggplant has softened slightly and is light golden, adding a little more oil as necessary. Add to the slow cooker.

- Heat another tablespoon of oil in the pan, then cook the remaining eggplant in the same way. Add to the slow cooker.

- Heat another tablespoon oil in the pan, then add the capsicum and cook for 3–4 minutes, or until it starts to soften and brown, turning often. Add the Moroccan spice mix and mix to combine well. Cook, stirring, for 30 seconds, or until fragrant, then add 1 tin of tomatoes, stirring to loosen any stuck-on bits from the bottom of the pan.

- Transfer the mixture to the slow cooker. Add the remaining tomatoes, the tomato paste and the chickpeas and stir to combine well. Arrange the pumpkin on top of the mixture. Cover and cook on low for 4 hours, or until the vegetables are very tender but still holding their shape.

- Gently stir in the lemon juice, honey, olives and coriander. Season to taste with sea salt and freshly ground black pepper.

- Combine the yoghurt and mint. Serve the ratatouille on a bed of steamed rice, with the minted yoghurt and harissa.

Pulses & grains

LEBANESE LAMB STEW WITH BEANS

preparation time 20 minutes
cooking time 7 hours
serves 6

2 tablespoons plain (all-purpose) flour

2 teaspoons sea salt

½ teaspoon freshly ground black
    pepper

1 tablespoon baharat

1.5 kg (3 lb 5 oz) lamb shoulder,
    trimmed and cut into 3 cm
    (1¼ inch) chunks

2 tablespoons tomato paste
    (concentrated purée)

125 ml (4 fl oz/½ cup) tomato passata
    (puréed tomatoes)

1 onion, finely chopped

2 garlic cloves, crushed

400 g (14 oz/2 cups) basmati rice

400 g (14 oz) tin white beans, rinsed
    and drained

1 handful coriander (cilantro) leaves

lemon cheeks, to serve

thinly shaved cucumber, to serve

baby English spinach leaves, to serve

- Place the flour, salt, pepper and baharat in a large bowl. Add the lamb and toss until evenly coated, then place the lamb in a slow cooker.

- Add the tomato paste, passata, onion, garlic, and 125 ml (4 fl oz/½ cup) water and stir until well combined. Clean the sides of the cooker with a damp cloth if necessary. Cover and cook on low for 6–7 hours, or until the lamb is very tender and breaks apart when stirred.

- Meanwhile, near serving time, prepare the rice. Rinse the rice under cold running water until the water runs clear. Place the rice and 375 ml (13 fl oz/ 1½ cups) cold water in a large saucepan, then cover and cook over low heat for 20–25 minutes, or until the rice is tender.

- Add the white beans to the slow cooker and gently stir in. Cover and cook for a further 10 minutes to heat through.

- Divide the lamb among serving bowls and garnish with the coriander. Serve with the rice, lemon cheeks, cucumber and baby spinach.

Note *Baharat is a spice mixture used in Middle Eastern cooking. It is available in specialty stores and Middle Eastern supermarkets. Although there is no direct substitute, you can use any Middle Eastern spice mix in this stew. Instead of rice, you could also serve this stew with steamed couscous.*

ABRUZZI-STYLE LAMB WITH BEANS

preparation time 25 minutes
cooking time 7 hours 10 minutes
serves 6

2 red capsicums (peppers)
400 g (14 oz) tin chopped tomatoes
1.5 kg (3 lb 5 oz) leg of lamb,
    trimmed of any visible fat
2 onions, thinly sliced
2 garlic cloves, finely chopped
1 tablespoon tomato paste
    (concentrated purée)
a pinch of sugar
2 small rosemary sprigs
3 oregano sprigs
125 ml (4 fl oz/½ cup) white wine
125 ml (4 fl oz/½ cup) good-quality
    chicken stock
2 tablespoons roughly chopped
    flat-leaf (Italian) parsley

thyme sprigs, to garnish
cooked cannellini beans, to serve
steamed asparagus, to serve

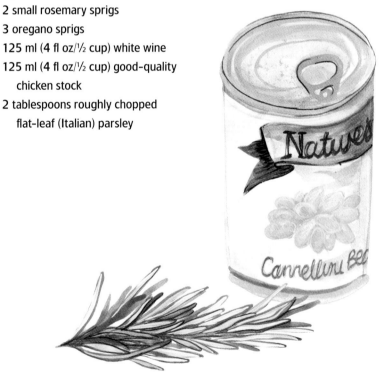

- Preheat the grill (broiler) to high.

- Cut the capsicums into quarters and remove the seeds and membranes. Place them on the grill tray, skin side up. Grill (broil) for 5–10 minutes, or until the skins have blistered and blackened. Place the capsicum in a bowl, cover and allow to cool. Peel off the skin and cut the flesh into thin strips. Set aside.

- In a blender or food processor, purée the tomatoes until smooth.

- Place the lamb in a slow cooker. Add the capsicum, puréed tomatoes, onion, garlic, tomato paste, sugar, rosemary and oregano sprigs. In a cup or small bowl, mix together the wine and stock. Pour over the lamb and stir together gently. Cover and cook on low for 3½ hours.

- Carefully turn the lamb over, then cover and cook for a further 3½ hours — the lamb should be falling off the bone.

- Carefully remove the lamb from the slow cooker and place on a chopping board. Carve into thick slices.

- Season the sauce in the slow cooker with sea salt and freshly ground black pepper to taste.

- Serve the lamb drizzled with the sauce and garnished with thyme sprigs, with cannellini beans and steamed asparagus on the side.

SPICY SAUSAGE AND BEAN CASSEROLE

preparation time 20 minutes
cooking time 7½ hours
serves 6

300 g (10½ oz/1½ cups) dried
   cannellini beans
300 g (10½ oz/1⅓ cups) dried
   black-eyed beans
6 bacon slices, cut into 6 cm
   (2½ inch) lengths
4 small onions, quartered
10 garlic cloves, peeled

3 long thin carrots, cut into 3 cm
   (1¼ inch) pieces
3 bay leaves
7 oregano sprigs, leaves only
1 small red chilli, split and seeded
500 ml (17 fl oz/2 cups) chicken stock
2 tablespoons tomato paste
   (concentrated purée)
6 thick pork sausages

• Soak the beans in a large saucepan of water overnight. Drain, discarding
the water, then put the beans in a saucepan with fresh water, bring to the boil
and boil rapidly for 10 minutes. Rinse and drain again.

• Layer the bacon over the base of the slow cooker. Add the onion, garlic
cloves, carrot, bay leaves, half the oregano and the chilli and season well
with freshly ground black pepper. Pour in the cannellini and black-eyed beans.

• Combine the stock and tomato paste and pour over the beans. Season
with freshly ground black pepper. Cook on high for 6 hours, then add the
sausages and cook for a further 1½ hours, or until the beans are tender
and the sausages are cooked through.

• Stir and taste for seasoning. Sprinkle the remaining oregano into
the casserole just before serving.

PORK AND RICE HOTPOT

preparation time 20 minutes
cooking time 3 hours
serves 4

500 g (1 lb) lean pork fillet
15 g (½ oz) dried Chinese
   mushrooms, sliced
300 g (10 oz/1½ cups) long-grain rice
1½ tablespoons hoisin sauce
2 teaspoons grated fresh ginger
3 garlic cloves, crushed
1 cinnamon stick
2 star anise
2 tablespoons dark soy sauce

1 tablespoon light soy sauce
2 tablespoons Chinese rice wine
500 ml (17 fl oz/2 cups) good-quality
   chicken stock
140 g (5 oz) tinned straw mushrooms,
   rinsed and drained
125 g (4½ oz) tinned sliced bamboo
   shoots, drained
shredded spring onions (scallions),
   to garnish

● Cut the pork into 2 cm (¾ inch) cubes. Put the pork, dried mushrooms, rice, hoisin sauce, ginger, garlic, cinnamon stick, star anise, dark and light soy sauces, rice wine, stock, straw mushrooms and bamboo shoots in the slow cooker.

● Cook on low for 3 hours, or until the rice and pork are cooked and the stock is absorbed.

● Divide the pork and rice among serving bowls, garnish with spring onions and serve with steamed Asian greens.

Pulses & grains

181

ARMENIAN CHICKEN WITH RICE PILAF

preparation time 25 minutes
cooking time 4–5 hours
serves 4

cooking oil spray
1.2 kg (2 lb 10 oz) chicken
1 lemon
2 garlic cloves, lightly crushed
3 thyme sprigs
2 teaspoons olive oil
¼ teaspoon paprika

RICE PILAFF
200 g (7 oz/1 cup) par-cooked
   long-grain rice
50 g (1¾ oz) vermicelli, broken into
   small pieces
40 g (1½ oz/¼ cup) pine nuts
30 g (1 oz) butter, melted
500 ml (17 fl oz/2 cups) chicken stock

- Spray the slow cooker bowl with cooking oil spray or grease well with butter or oil.

- Wash the chicken and pat dry with paper towel. Finely grate the zest from half of the lemon and set the zest aside. Cut the lemon into quarters. Stuff the chicken with the lemon quarters, garlic and thyme. Skewer or tie the legs and wings together with kitchen string, then place the chicken, breast side up, in the slow cooker.

- Brush the chicken breast and legs with the olive oil and sprinkle over the paprika, some salt and freshly ground black pepper. Cook on high for 1 hour.

- Meanwhile, to make the rice pilaff, put the rice, vermicelli and pine nuts in a large bowl and stir through the butter and reserved lemon zest, then add the chicken stock. Carefully pour this around the chicken in the slow cooker, distributing it evenly around and mixing the rice and vermicelli into the liquid.

- Cook on high for a further 3–4 hours, or until the rice is cooked and the chicken is tender and the juices run clear when the thigh is pierced with a skewer. Stir the rice with a fork once or twice during cooking.

- Lift the chicken carefully from the slow cooker and remove the skewers or string. Cut or pull the chicken apart into large pieces. Serve with the rice pilaff and a salad or steamed vegetables.

Pulses & grains

MEXICAN CHICKEN

preparation time 10 minutes
cooking time 4 hours
serves 4

cooking oil spray
600 g (1 lb 5 oz) boneless, skinless
 chicken thighs
330 g (11½ oz/1½ cups)
 par-cooked short-grain rice
400 g (14 oz) tinned red kidney
 beans, drained and rinsed

400 g (14 oz) jar spicy taco sauce
250 ml (9 fl oz/1 cup) chicken stock
250 g (9 oz/2 cups) grated cheddar
 cheese
125 g (4½ oz/½ cup) sour cream
1 handful coriander (cilantro) leaves,
 chopped

● Spray the slow cooker bowl with cooking oil spray or grease well with butter or oil.

● Trim the chicken of excess fat and cut each thigh in half. Put the rice in the base of the slow cooker and top with the chicken pieces, kidney beans, taco sauce, stock and cheese. Cook on low for 4 hours, or until the chicken and rice are tender.

● Serve the chicken topped with a dollop of sour cream and garnish with chopped coriander.

DRUNKEN CHICKEN WITH RICE

preparation time 15 minutes
cooking time 3 hours
serves 4

1.6 kg (3 lb 8 oz) chicken
2 slices fresh ginger
2 garlic cloves, squashed
2 spring onions (scallions), trimmed
1 star anise
250 g (9 oz/1¼ cups) par-cooked
  long-grain rice

250 ml (9 fl oz/1 cup) Chinese rice
  wine
250 ml (9 fl oz/1 cup) good-quality
  chicken stock
light soy sauce, to serve

• Trim the excess fat from the cavity of the chicken. Put the ginger, garlic, spring onions and star anise in the cavity.

• Put the rice in the base of the slow cooker. Pour over the rice wine and stock and place the chicken on the top. Cook on high for 3 hours, or until the rice is cooked and the chicken juices run clear when the thigh is pierced with a skewer. Serve drizzled with light soy sauce.

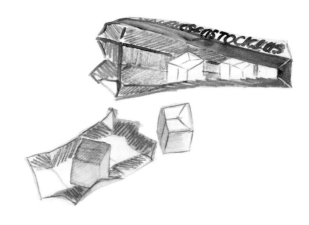

Index

Index

Index